I0798535

How to Create Art Without Knowing How to Draw a Straight Line

By Arlene Wright-Correll

Original illustrations and paintings are all copyrighted and created

By Arlene Wright-Correll

Cover artwork by Arlene Wright-Correll
“Stokes Baird Round Barn©” 2006

Other books by this author

The Bakers Dozen©

Who’s who in KY Arts and Crafts© 2006 Edition

The Impractical Gardener©

Take That Old Car Out of Your Front Yard and Plant a Garden©

You can find them at http://stores.lulu.com/kate1031

ISBN # 978-0-6151-5184-7

Publications Trade Resources Unlimited

100 Dave Wintsch Rd., Munfordville, KY 42765

Forward

I firmly believe that we come into this world knowing everything we need to know! (How about "a little child shall lead them") Then we spend the next 4 or 5 years with our chosen parents, who thinking they are doing us some good, proceed to deprogram us to what they think is normal. Very few of us survive this crisis.

It continues on in the lower grades in school. Lord forbid you should draw a tree with leaves and use your blue crayons to color the trunk and your red crayons to color the leaves. This would be "wrong" since everyone knows that trunks are brown and leaves are green. Yet if you really, really look at a trunk of a tree you will see shades of brown, black, grey, green, yellow and blue in the bark and perhaps you were coloring your picture in autumn which is when school usually starts and the trees are red and gold and yellow and orange, but the drawing plan in the teachers book is brown and green and you are told you failed kindergarten art 101, so you put your crayons away and rarely take them out again to be truly creative. You go through life saying, "But I can't even draw a straight line" without realizing there are many things are painted and drawn that have no straight lines!

So here's to you, all of you who failed Kindergarten art 101. I am going to show you how to paint without knowing how to "Draw a Straight line"… I am going to share some real trade secrets that will start you on having the best time of your life letting your creative juices flow. They never died, they just went to sleep. This is your first step to stretching and growing regardless of how old or young you are.

This book is dedicated to Donna Wright-Ace my oldest daughter who is taking the time in her life to finally let her creative juices flow.

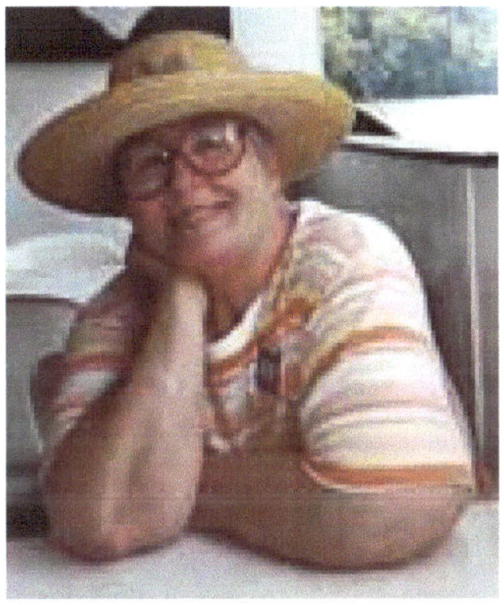

About the Author & Artist. Arlene Wright-Correll (1935-___), popular American award winning Artist, author & avid gardener, at the age of 68, decided to pick up her paint brushes again after 54 years and paint, in mostly gouache watercolors and pastels, the flowers, herbs and fruits that grow at Home Farm Herbery in Munfordville, KY.

Though she paints in all mediums, she likes to use the Gouache paints, which are a heavy, opaque watercolor paint, sometimes called body color, producing a less wet-appearing and more strongly colored picture than ordinary watercolor. Occasionally, she will paint something from her world travels especially of Scotland, Ireland, or the Mediterranean. She is fond of those old memories. She is the resident artist and workshop instructor at Avalon Stained Glass Studio.

She is also a **certified and juried member of the South Central KY Arts and Crafts Guild artist.** She is also the founder of said guild in 2005 and in 2007 she was elected president of the guild. She is a **Certified EBSQ artist** and a **nominated member to The Museum of Women's Art** in Washington, DC, KY Water Color Society

Ms. Wright-Correll is the creator and author of **Who's Who in KY Arts and Crafts** and a member of **KAHT.**
Exhibitions:
1st place winner Salis International, Colorado Springs, May 2005. Hydras Watercolors.
Artist of the Month, Horse Cave Book Store, 2006
She is one of the six chosen KY Artists who worked 6 months to create the dolls for Journey Jots in 2006.
Western KY University Celebration of the Arts, 2007
South Central KY Cultural Center, Glasgow KY, 2007
Women in the Arts, Bowling Green, KY 2007

Her original paintings are sold quite quickly and one can always try and pick up whatever current one she is working on. The amazing thing about this "young" artist is that as a mother of 5 & the grandmother of 5, she is also a cancer and stroke survivor who is able to strive forward each and everyday to welcome the beauty of this small planet. She is also a China & Porcelain painter, Stained Glass Artisan, Works in Fused Glass and Encaustic Art.

Her favorite motto is a quote by Ruth Smelter., "You have not lived a perfect day, even though you have earned your money, unless you have done something for someone who cannot repay you." http://www.avalonstainedglassschool.com/page/1228822

All paintings are by the award winning artist Arlene Wright-Correll. These and others can be seen by going to her website.

http://www.learn-america.com/stories/storyReader$158

Chapter 1

How to Paint without Knowing How to Draw a Straight Line

If I have heard this once, I have heard this a thousand times, "I can't even draw a straight line". I hear it every time someone looks at one of my paintings.

I basically feel one can paint or create art in any painting or drawing medium without knowing how to draw a straight line.

I can draw things if I work hard at it. Sometimes they look like they are supposed to and sometimes they don't! Being over 72 years old has made my drawing hand shaky more times than not.

It helps to know perspective, but that is very easy to learn. Fortunately for me I was an art major in high school, but never went anywhere with it. Then I did not do any art for 12 years. I was able to paint off and on again from1965 to 1967. I was unable to pick up a paint brush or pencil again until 1999. During that time, I forgot more than I remembered. Being on a very limited income in my old age did not allow me to take many art seminars or workshops. However, I was able to invest in books. When I saw a book I thought would teach me something and I felt it was not in my budget, I would get the ISP number and go to half.com or eBay and I usually could find it either used at a very low price or new at a very good discounted price.

At that time I found myself with more time to devote to this past time that I truly enjoyed. I started with oils again. Once into it, I found I could try other things I liked such as pen and ink sketches.

My philosophy in life has always been to stretch and grow. It was no different in this area. I started to try all things I had never done before, such oil pastels, soft pastels, hydro watercolors, watercolors, gouache watercolors.

I fell in love with watercolors. They were a fast and easy medium to learn. The paintings were done quickly or at least the paint dried faster than oils or acrylics.

I knew hardly anything about the medium, but I bought some books and within a year I was selling just about everything I painted.

I learned to paint what I know. Places I had been to, things around my home, painting things I liked to see. I painted for myself! I stretched to portraits and animals and frankly some of them were terrible, but eventually they started to look like they were supposed to look.

At this point you are thinking, "yeah, but you can draw a straight line!"

Let me introduce you to some trade secrets of today's artists.

I like to use the Graphic tracing paper method.

If one has a computer and scanner, one can scan the scene, picture or photo of what they want to paint. One can then enlarge it on a program such as Adobe Photoshop and print it down to the size they want. My printer lets me print as large as a tabloid size which is 13 x 17".

Then I get the paper or canvas I want to use and lay out a piece of graphite tracing paper. I put the printed image on top of it and using a stylus or a pencil I outline the areas I want to paint. I do not put in details. When I am done, I may work on the painting in any medium I want from oils to watercolors to pastels. I may put in different colors, or if I am doing something that I want to be the same as the photo I will use the printed image as a guide.

Many artists use a light box such as the ones I describe below. I have yet to use one.

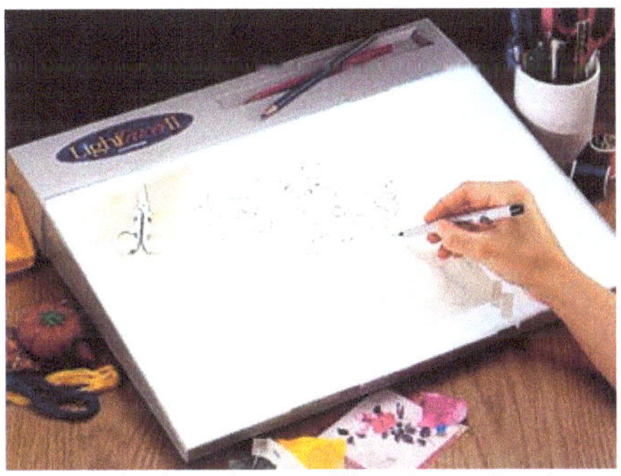

Good looking light boxes with an inclined working surface and special slot for holding drawing pens or pencils. Made of space age high impact plastic they are both portable and practical. Some come with a 10 x 12" viewing area and 8-watt daylight fluorescent bulb and run anywhere in price from $24.95 to $29.95. A nice one is Lightracer II with 12 x 18" viewing area illuminated by an 18", 15 watt daylight fluorescent bulb and runs about $89.00, but is often on sale in places like Jerry's Artarama for about $54.00. We have a large one of these in our stained glass studio and use it for patterns. One of these days I am going to try it. Whichever one you buy or make you must have it so it can show though up to 300 pound art paper. The one in the studio looks like this and it is set against the wall on an angle.

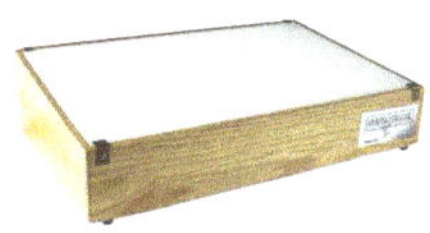

You can even make your own very easily by buying the light box top and the bulb and putting the wood around it.

For Making Any Picture Larger or Smaller you can use a Pantograph. They come in metal or wood. Special crisscross design of bars allows you to trace any design and enlarge or reduce it. All you do is trace with the tracer pin and automatically the design is transferred in perfect proportion to paper, board or canvas. With a Pantograph at your side, you can use any picture you may come across and blow up or

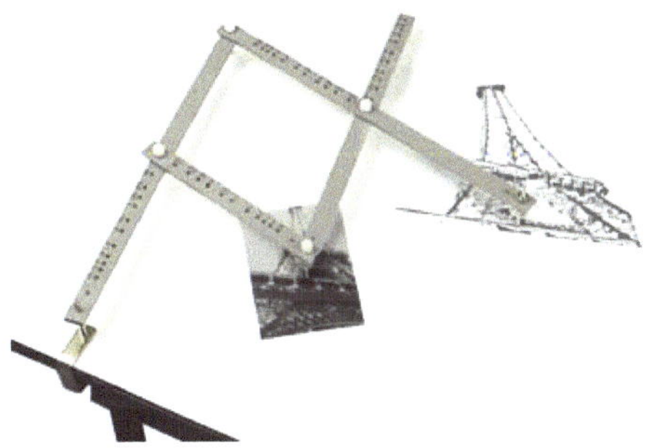

reduce it!

Pantographs cost $30.00 to $45.00 and can usually be found on sale.

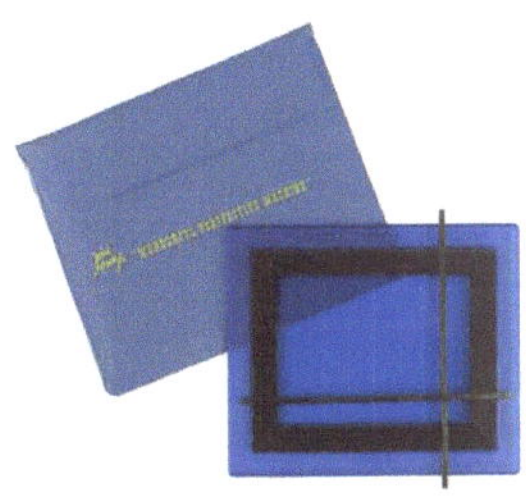

Another way is to grid what you want to paint by drawing equal lines horizontally and then vertically. Once you have done that you can do the same thing to whatever size canvas or paper you want to paint or draw on. Then just sketch in from box to box, sort of like filling in the numbers without numbers.

A guy named John Pike invented a perspective machine which is really cheap. Using traditional perspective drawing methodology John Pike created this easy to hold machine to make it easier than ever to accomplish. Just grid your canvas like the viewing grid. Then hold the machine at arm's length in front of the subject. Place the magnetic steel strips around key subject matter to aid in viewing. Then draw the grid on your canvas. It's that easy. It is 5x6" in size with carrying case.

I have never used one of this; however, I often use the grid method when I want to do portraits.

I finally invested in a prism projector. However, I have yet to use it. There are all different kinds and start as low as $50.00 and go on up. The best ones I have found, again, are on Jerry's Artarama site. However, I am sure there are plenty on eBay either new or used.

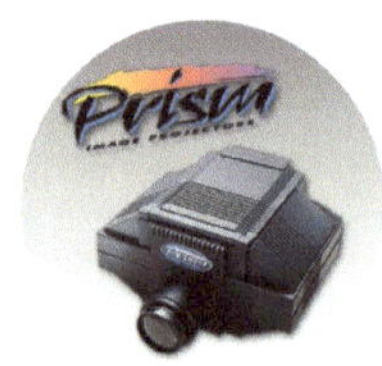

Here are a few you might want to investigate. The Prism has set the quality standard in artist quality opaque projectors for over ten years. It is one of three projectors in the Artograph range that we would recommend for projecting clear, color corrected and bright images onto wall, canvas, paper or board. This top loading projector features a 7x7" glass stage for you to place your original art, books or even small size 3-D objects on. It includes 500 watts (2-250 watt photo bulbs) of photo quality, color corrected incandescent light that provides crisp, bright white images. The bulbs last only about 25 hours so it is a good idea to have a couple of spare bulbs available. A cooling chamber keeps artwork cooler and helps avoid damage. Copy clips keeps art in position even when the unit is tilted while the dual magnetic latch keeps copy cover secure. With thermal overload protection. Prism's 225mm f/4.8 lens provides you with a horizontal projection range of up to 20x original size and reduction ability of up to 80% of the original size by simply reversing the lens. Weighs just 8lbs allowing for easy movement in the studio and simple transport.

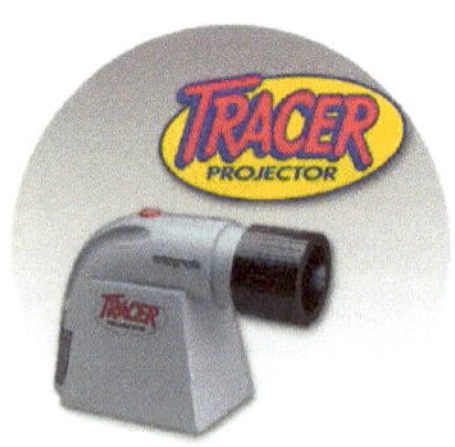

A real simple one is the trace projector. A surprisingly inexpensive way to enlarge art, photos, designs and 3D objects for sizing and tracing - getting you to the fun part faster. This bottom loading projector will accept full size copy up to 5x5" in size or larger copy in sections and all small 3-D items. It enlarges up to 10x size in full color onto wall, board or canvas.

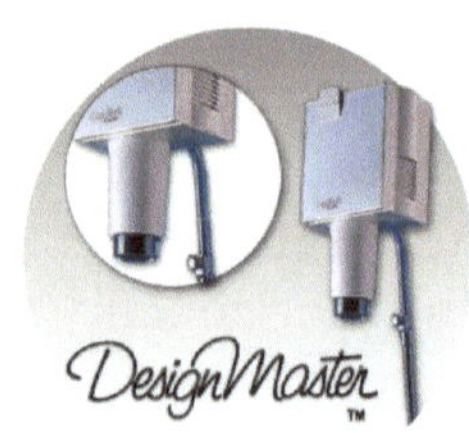

THE PERFECT PROJECTOR FOR THE WATERCOLORIST AND DESIGNER! It is made to project vertically down onto work, drawing or drafting table. It comes equipped with an adjustable vertical stand that easily clamps to any table surface up to 2 inches thick. Original designs and patterns up to 6x6" can be projected onto table top from a reduction size of 70% of original to a 4x enlargement of originals in just a matter of seconds. Two adjustable magnetic copy clips keep originals securely in place. You can also remove this projector from the stand for enlarging up to 30x original size (15 x15 feet!) onto wall or canvas for producing murals, banners, signs or any large graphics. The 250-watt photo bulb provides for bright and clear images. The bulbs last just 25 hours so an additional bulb would be a good idea to have on hand to use just attach stand to your drawing board or work table, mount design or photo into the convenient magnetic copy board, adjust to desired size, focus and trace image. Images are sharp and bright. With black housing, powerful fan for cool operation, front loading 6x6" magnetic hinged copy board, 250-watt bulb and 200mm high quality ground glass lens. UL approved. They start at about $150.00 and go up.

Doing anything well is just a matter of practice, drill and rehearse! One cannot take piano lessons and expect to sound great unless one practices, drills and rehearses. The same thing applies to creating works of art.

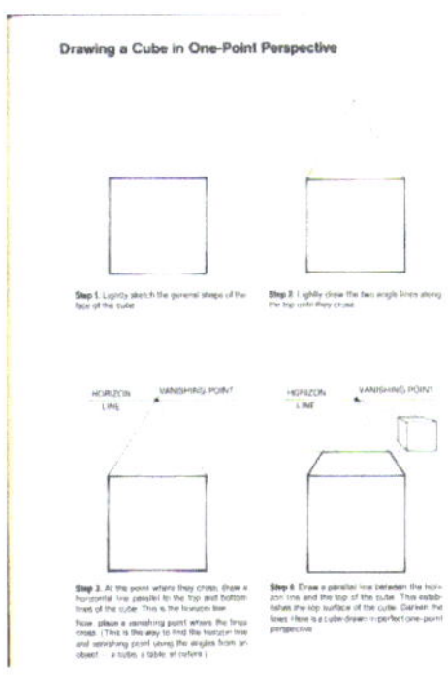

Let's start with drawing in perspective. There is a great little book titled "Perspective" by William F. Powell and it is published by Walter Foster who publishes tons of art books. I heartily recommend this book and all others by Walter Foster. I have found them very inexpensively listed on www.half.com and eBay.

When you practice use the cheapest paper you can find such as butcher's paper or what is called newspaper stock which is available at any art store.

Buy a cheap small sketchbook and keep practicing and practicing. Soon those little squares might look like this. Practice cones, circles, rectangles in perspective and you will wind up with some nice little, happy paintings.

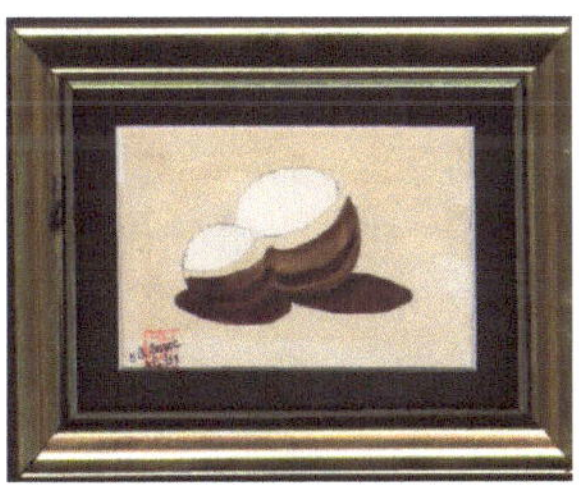
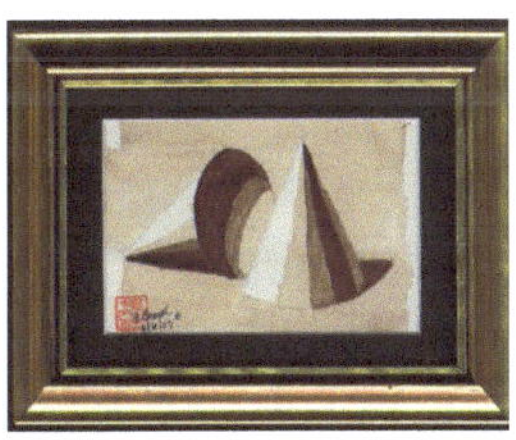
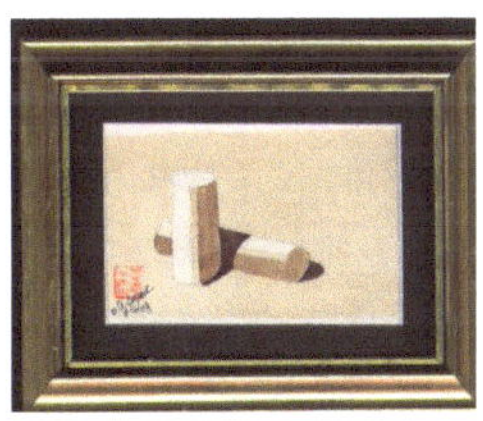
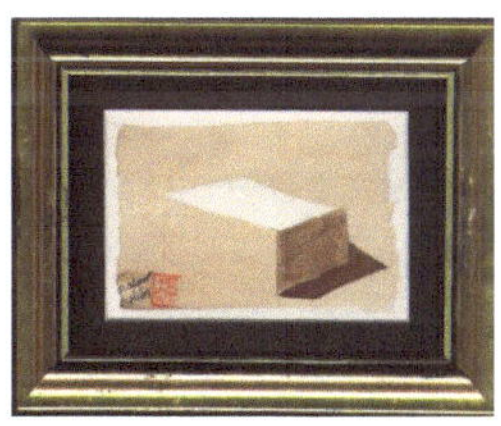

Don't be afraid of the nomenclature! Those are the big words that are indicative of any genre of anything. Read everything you can. What you do not understand, look it up on Google. So much free information!

If you don't want anyone to see or know what you are doing, then don't tell them or show them. However, a mentor or a cheering section is always good to have provided you ask them for their honest opinion and don't have a thin skin when you get it. Don't be afraid of failure. Just remember that Van Gogh never sold a painting in his life time! Renoir gave his away for as low as 50 cents just to have enough money to buy some more paint.

Start with something simple. Watercolors are so simple. They get a bad rap because some people think if you are not painting in oils, you are not an artist. I love watercolors because I can clean up quickly, I can hurry up a drying process with a hand held hair dryer, I can even remove paint, I can build up layers upon layers, I can leave white spaces. The gouache (pronounced g-wash) water colors give really brilliant colors. Here are some paintings that sold as quickly as I put them on eBay. They were painted right after I returned from a trip to the Mediterranean. They were all digital photos I had taken on our trip and I printed them out and painted from the photos.

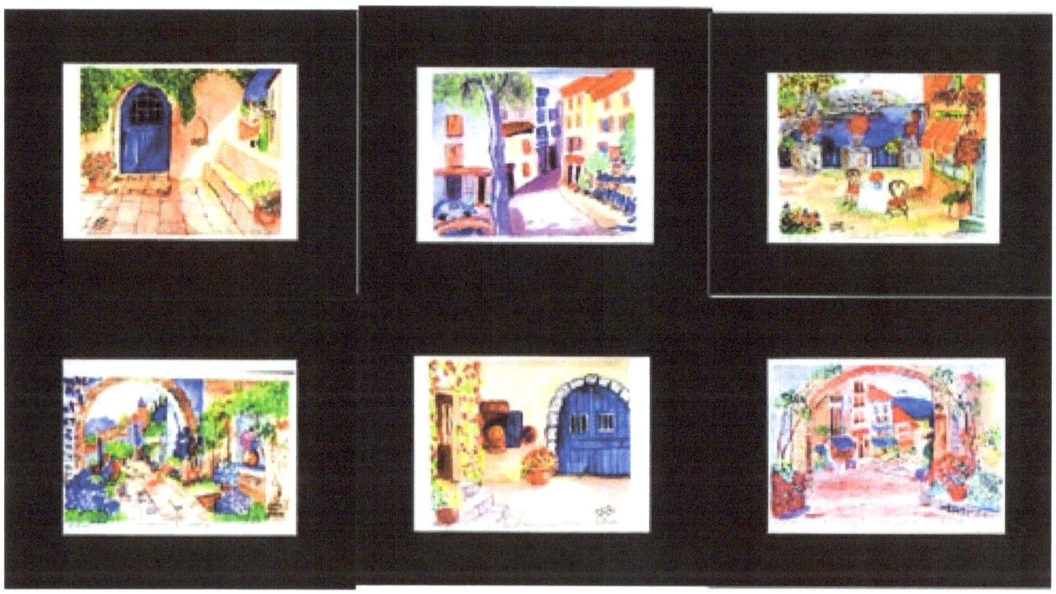

When I returned, this year, from Spain I wanted to do a sort of pictorial diary and I created the "Spanish Sketch Book or The 4 Amigos Go to Spain©". All the paintings started with photos either taken by my brother, George or myself. All the photos only had 3 of us in them at one time, so when I found a photo that had a good memory, and it was taken by George, I would paint George in and visa versa when I was taking the photo.

Remember part of the title is The 4 Amigos go to Spain. I would basically cut and paste on my computer what I wanted to see in the final drawing. Also because this was a sketchbook and I wanted it to be fun, I did not want a lot of detail. Most of my little drawings were done in the graphic tracing method and then I did water color washes and outlined in pen and ink.

When I was finished, not only was everyone delighted, I was delighted and had a great deal of satisfaction. Here are a couple of them. You can see all of them at my website. www.learn-america.com/stories/storyReader$158

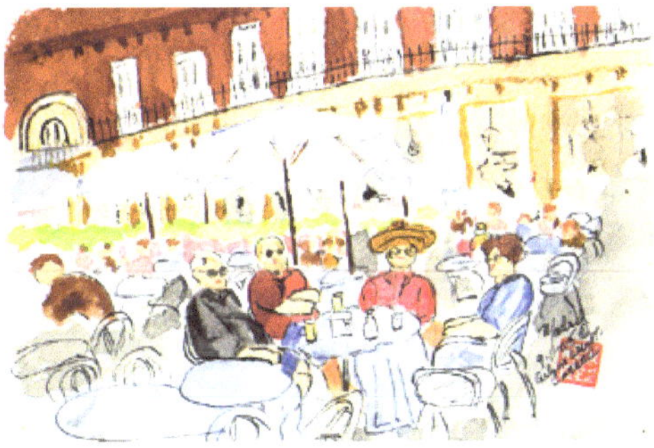

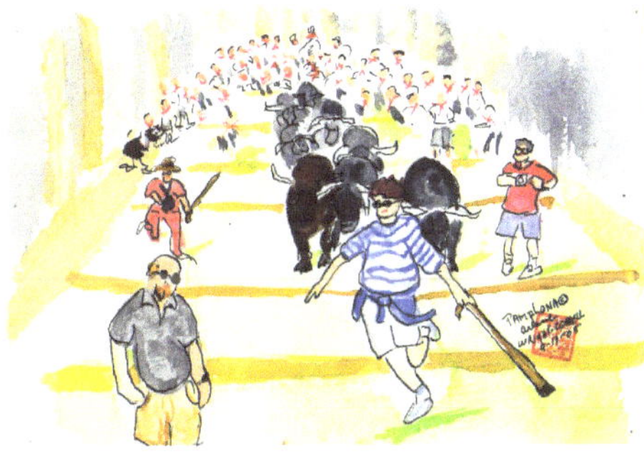

I think I did 14 or 15 little paintings that immediately brings pleasant memories of our trip, tells a part of the story and we are each identifiable by our clothing. As you can see they are nothing grand, but all tell a whole story with the paintings and the little diary has received a lot of positive comments from friends and families.

When I started painting again in 1999 I did one oil painting in a 6 month time. In the winter of 2000 I did another oil painting. In 2001 I discovered watercolors. I have painted over 200 paintings since that date up to November 2005. I have also tried oil pastels which I like very much. Here is one I did with that medium.

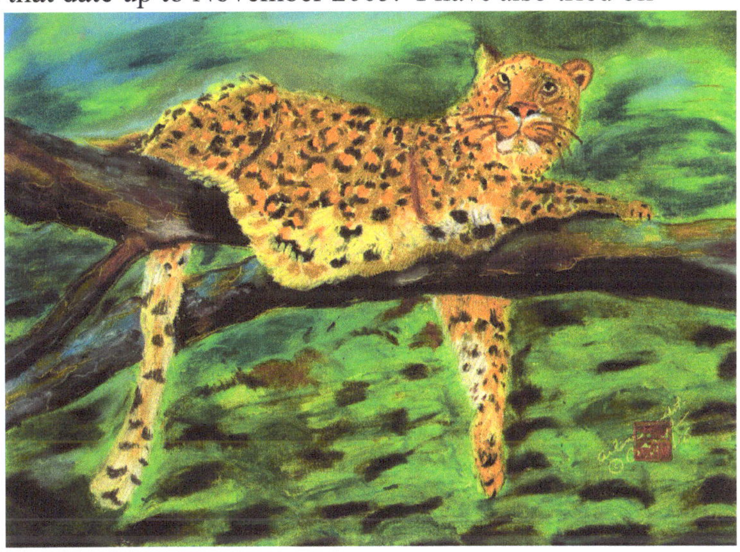

That led me to soft pastels which are a total delight.

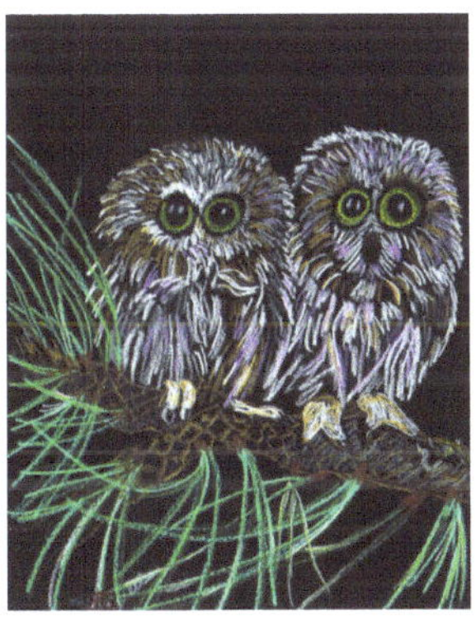

As you can see in "Who's Whoo?" it is nothing but a series of lines that created a great little picture of these Saw Wet Owls.

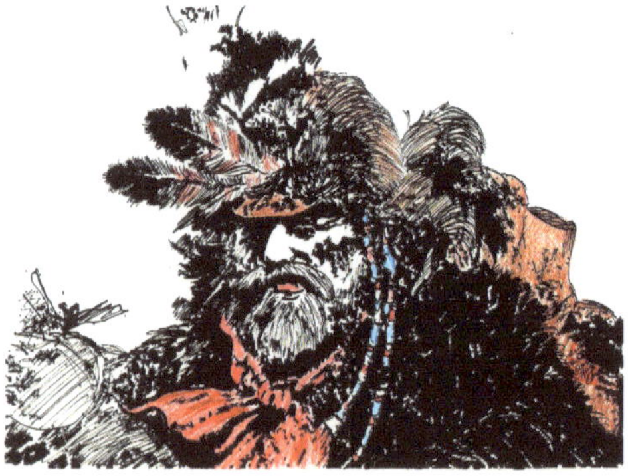

Pen and Ink is a fun medium and occasionally I do something with those. One can do something elaborate with lines and a watercolor wash as in "Mountain Man" to the left or something simple such as "Hard to Kill" to the right.

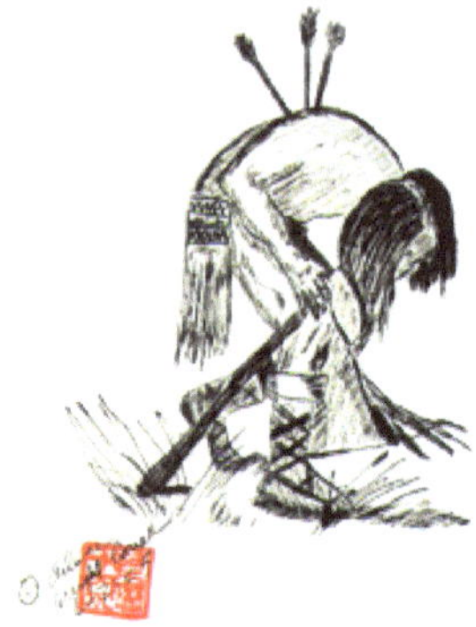

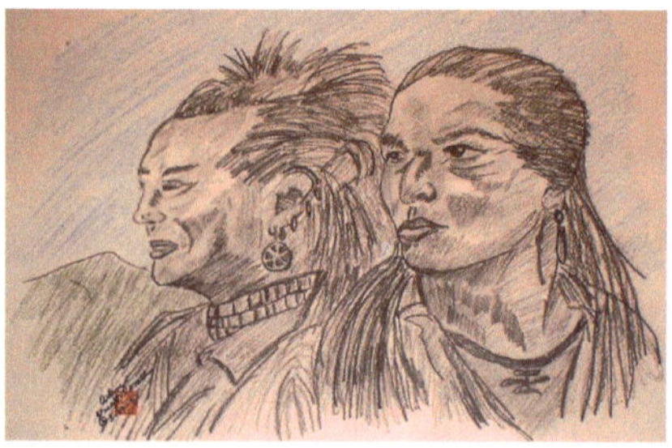

Just remember, practice, drill and rehearse. I try to paint or draw at least 2 hours a day. Sometimes I will do it for much longer. It depends on how my life is going. Sadly, there are some days I do not get to paint or draw at all.

On the left is a drawing titled, "The Last of the Mohicans" and it was done as a practice drawing and lo and behold someone thought it was great and bought it for a friend as a Christmas gift.

Many times I have finished something that I thought was not my best and others have loved them and bought them. Such as the "Grand Canal" that went to Houston, TX and the "Lavender Fields" that went somewhere else.

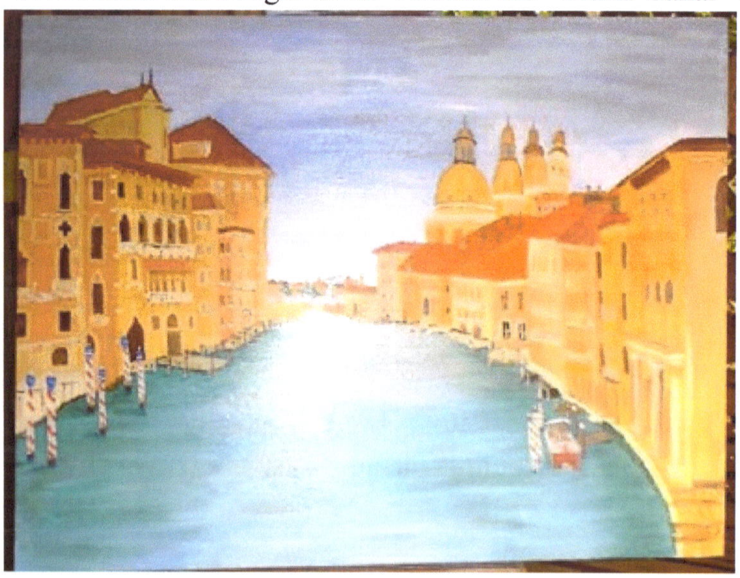

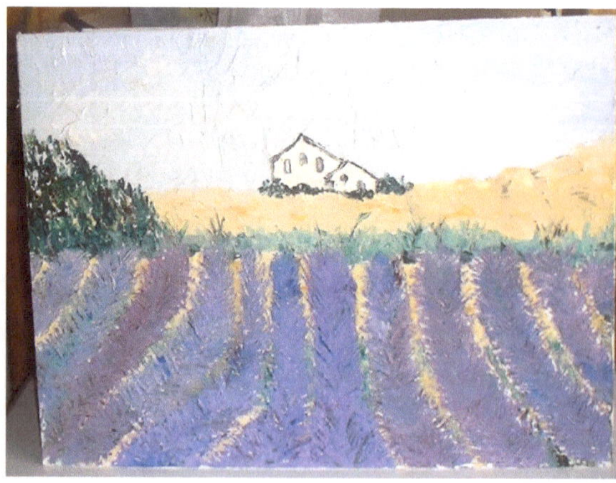

The "Grand Canal" was a very large oil painting done of a place we visited one year. The "Lavender Field" was an oil painting done with a palette knife. I had put them both on my website and put them in the garage and they sat there for almost 2 years before someone bought them. So you never can tell. Art, like Beauty, is in the eye of the beholder!

Don't be afraid to enter contests. I tried Hydrous Watercolors and did a picture in April 2005. I learned the manufacturer had an art contest. I was entry # 931 and this painting done with their product on a large canvas board won 1st place. I was floored and delighted when they told me "Coming Down to the Wire" was their 1st place winner.

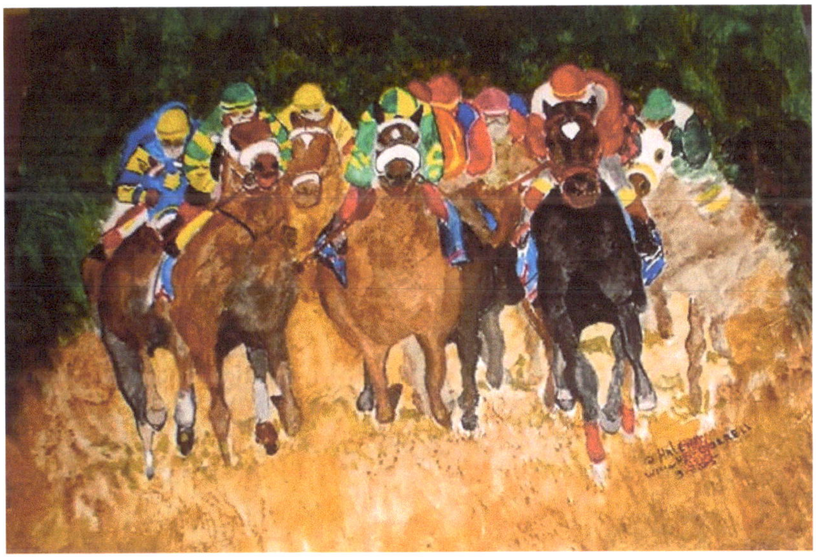

Many contests have a student or beginner's category.

Subscribe to art magazines. Go to art shows and museums. If you could walk into the Louvre or any other big art museum and you will often see people with easels in front of famous paintings copying the style of the old masters.

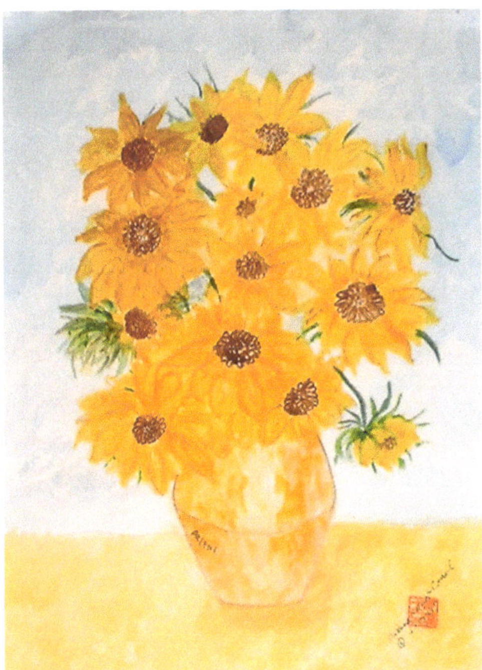

I recently did this one called "Van Gogh Comes to Munfordville" in soft pastels. It was a fun exercise.

Again, practice, drill and rehearse.

Your initial investment in teaching yourself how to draw or paint could be done for as little as $25.00! You don't need tons of equipment and fancy paper etc. You just need to have the "D" word. Desire!

As you grow, so will your desire and soon you may find yourself with a gratifying hobby that might at least pay for your supplies and help you grow towards other things.
Join a local art society. If you had a chance to play golf with Arnold Palmer or Joe Duffer, who would you choose? Arnold, of course! Learn

from the pros. They had to learn it from someone. Your local art society welcomes beginners because all of us were beginners at one time or another. If you don't have one, start one. I put out the call in February of 2005 and founded the thriving South Central KY Arts and Crafts Guild.

You never can tell where this might take you. I never thought that one day I would have a studio built for me, but I have a nice little space that allows me to do what I like to do best. I know one 84 year old lady that cleaned out a big double door closet and put all her art supplies, easel etc in there and that is her "studio".

Make the time to start on your art adventure now. One never knows how short life can be. I was a widow when I was 22 years old. I am the mother of a son who unexpectedly died at the age of 40 years old and another who died at the age of 45. These three people left a lot of things undone in their life.

My grandmother used to say to me constantly. "Don't put off to tomorrow, what you can do today!" Now I am saying the same thing to you.

I realized many years ago that older people say things like, "I wished I'd learned that when I was a kid". Well, I'll let you in on a secret. The reason most kids learn so quickly is that most of them have no fear of failing! Don't worry about failing. No one is going to take you out behind the barn and shoot you.

Create a bio for yourself, business cards with your picture on it, Get something that is definitely "you" for your art, such as my Chinese Red Chop that is my whole name in Chinese. In China a signature is not legal unless it has a Chop over it.

I like the idea and had someone in China make me one and I now sign all my paintings that way.

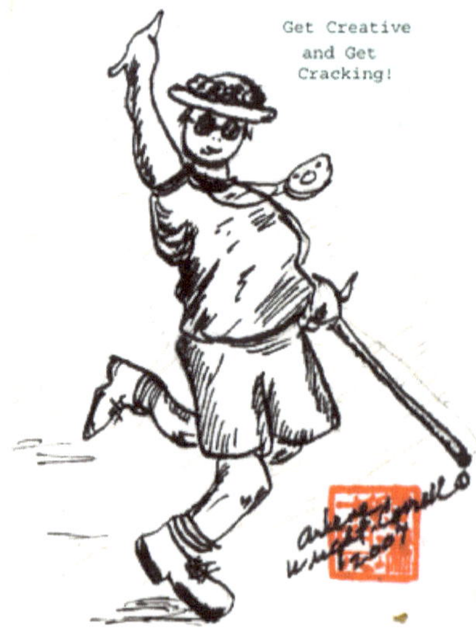

Chapter 2

How to Do Ukrainian Egg Painting

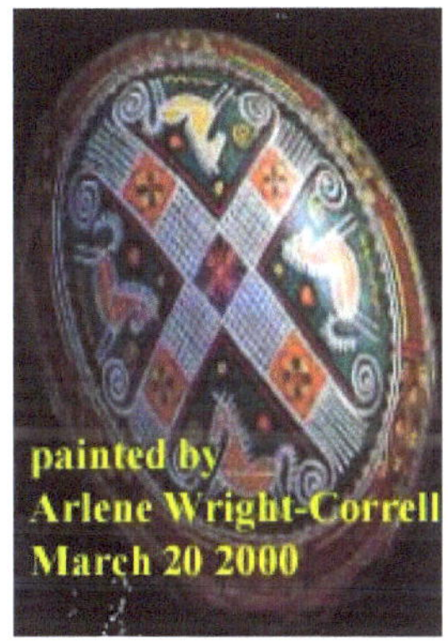

A couple of years ago I read how my Pen Pal Leonie, in Australia, had a miserable failure coloring her Easter eggs with a wax process. Well, the Calvary has arrived, Leonie. I decorate eggs using the Ukrainian Egg Painting method. Now this is a lot of work, dear heart, so if you intend to do an egg, think twice or 102 times about doing it just to look nice, then crack off the shell and eat the egg!

Ukrainian Egg Painting is called, "Pysanky" the Ukrainian folk art of egg decorating which follows at tradition over 2000 years old. In the craft, the artist begins with a raw white egg, symbol of life and rebirth. Using heated beeswax, designs are drawn onto the shell, and the egg is placed in a series of dye baths. The design is progressive with additions after each dye color. When the design is completed, the wax is removed, polyurethane protection is added, and the raw egg is blown from the shell.

An egg can take many hours to complete and is a treasure for years to come.

Ukrainian Egg symbols and colors have special meanings.

Yellow denotes youth, happiness, and love.

Light blue denotes sky with its life-giving air and good health.

Red indicates sun, happiness in life, hope and passion.

Orange is for the everlasting sun.

Brown represents mother earth bringing forth her bounty.

Pink indicates success.

Light green denotes breaking of shackles and freedom of bondage.

Dark red represents harvest, gathering fruit in the fall.

Purple is for faith, patience and trust.

Black indicates eternity, darkest time before dawn.

The following symbol picture is from my first class which I found offered for $12.00 in the Vero Beach, FL library January or February of 1999 and I am sharing it with you.

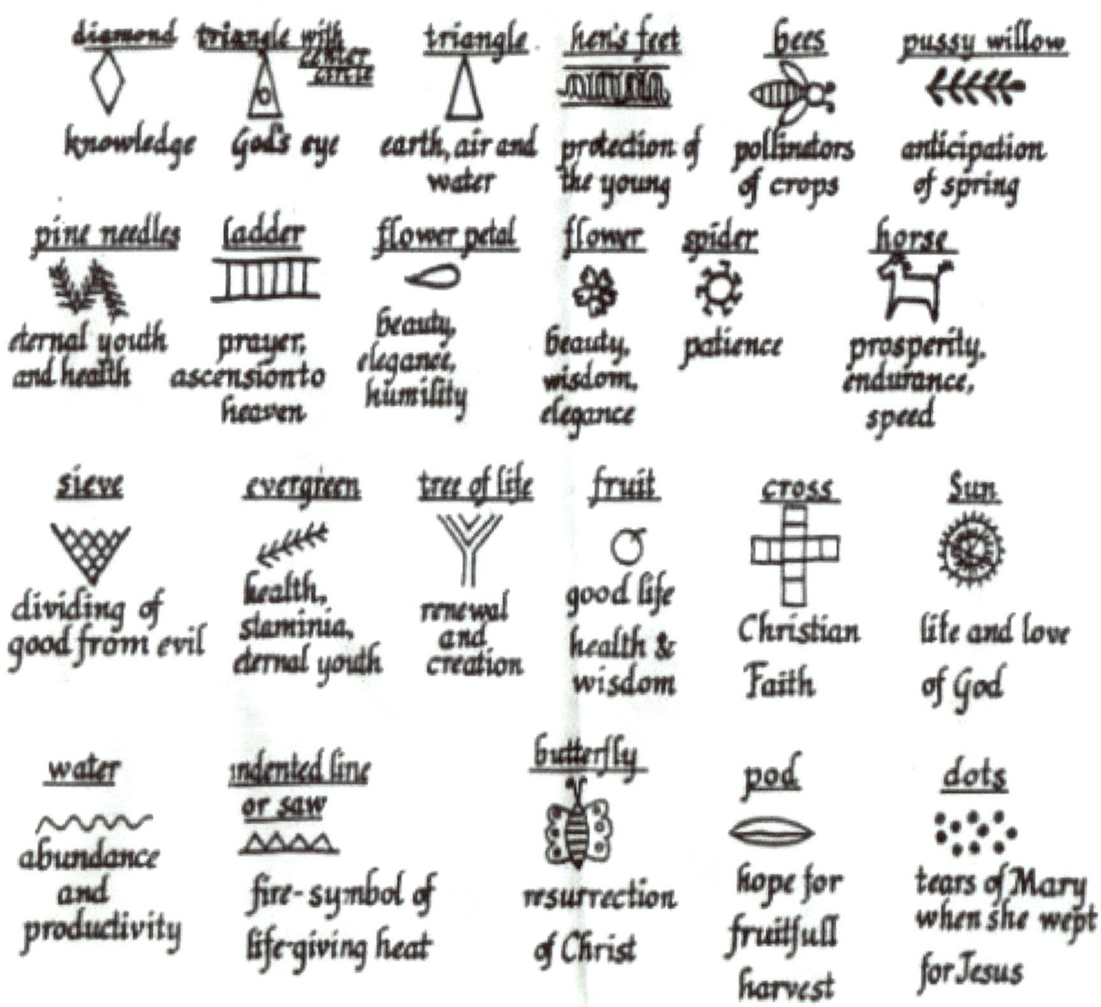

There are some simple tools you will need and I am providing a list of them for you. Plus the instructions are quite simple also.

1. First you need to protect your worktable with a few layers of newspapers. Keep some paper towel sheets in a small stack nearby. Make sure you have a good light source so your eggs are not in the shadows.

2. When shopping for eggs suitable for Pysanky, the best source is to get unwashed eggs directly from an egg farm. Let just laid eggs stand 4 or 5 days before decorating. If you buy your eggs from the store, they may not take the dye because they are washed in strong solutions. What I do is get my eggs from the super market and let them stand for 3 hours in a solution of 2 tablespoons of white vinegar and one quart of tepid water. Do not use jumbo or extra large eggs as they tend to have weaker shells.

3. Work on eggs that are room temperature.

Some people blow their eggs prior to working on them. I prefer to complete the egg and then blow out the egg.

4. The tools needed are quite simple and inexpensive.

The one tool is called a Kistky. I originally learned this craft with a brass kistka and I personally prefer the electric Kistky. The diagrams below are from my first class and I am sharing them with you so you know what they look like.

I. Candle heated kistky

1. Traditional kistka - handmade, comes in fine, medium, and heavy sizes. This tool has been used for many years. It has a brass funnel wound with copper wire and a wooden handle.

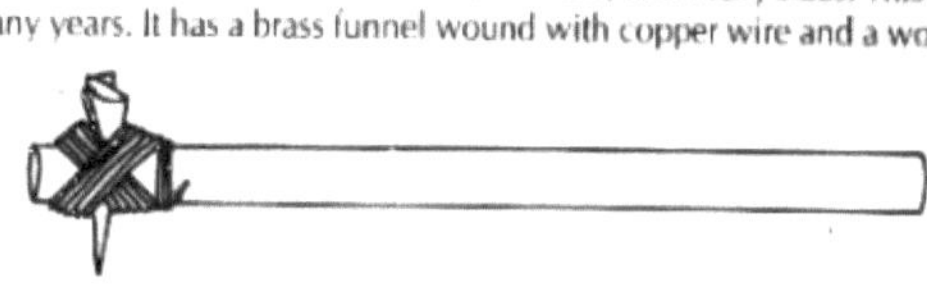

2. Brass kistka - precision tooled, available in fine, medium, and heavy sizes. It has a brass tip and a delrin (plastic) handle.

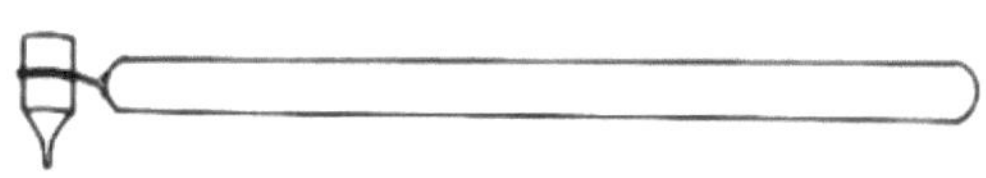

II. Electric kistky

1. Stationary tip kistky - comes in sizes extra-fine, fine, medium, heavy, and extra-heavy. The tips are not removable except for replacement.

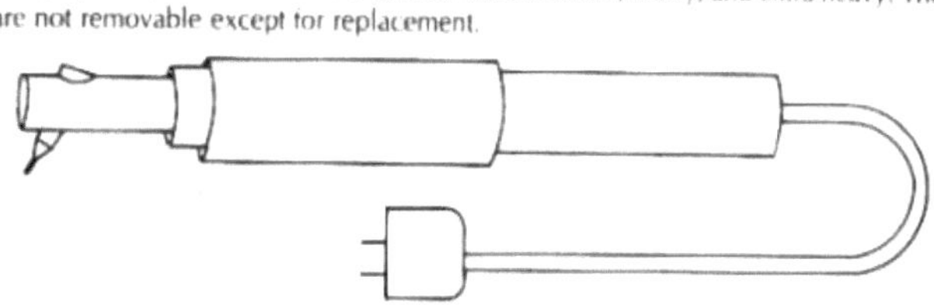

2. Interchangeable kistka - comes in fine, medium, and heavy. An extra-fine and extra-heavy tip can be purchased separately.

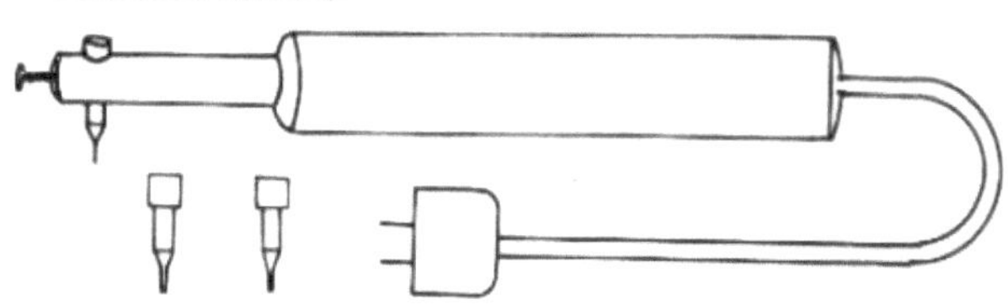

You will need fine, medium, and heavy kistky to make the eggs in this book. For more intricate eggs, you may also use an extra-fine kistka.

2

5. Beeswax seals the color of the surface it covers. Pure beeswax is the only type of wax used in this egg dying process. Regular light beeswax is used with kistky, which are heated in the candle flame. This wax will gradually turn black from the carbon in the flame. I buy darkened beeswax, which I use in the electric kistky with the interchangeable tips, as it is needed to see the design and areas being filled in. One of the last steps in decorating Pysanky is to remove the wax, which allows the colors beneath it to reappear.

When one is not using an electric kistky, then a candle in a secure holder is needed to heat the traditional or brass kistky. **Never use candle wax to decorate the egg.**

6. A number 2 or 3 pencil is used when dividing the egg at the beginning. These pencil lines will not show on the egg providing you have drawn them lightly. Do not erase your lines as the dye will not take to the shell in that area.

7. Use stainless steel spoons for dipping the eggs in and out of the dye. I use a little Chinese wire egg "catcher/dipper" that is used in Manchurian Firepots and can be found in an oriental market for under $2.00.

8. A Q-tip or a small paintbrush is used to add dye to small areas.

9. The paper towels are used to pat the eggs dry when they come out of the dye. The longer you leave the egg in the dye, the darker the color will be.

10. White vinegar is added to most of the dyes to keep them strong.

11. Varnish adds protection and luster and a clear fast, drying glossy varnish or polyurethane wood finish is what I use. Do not use water-soluble varnish as it causes the dyes to run.

12. I keep waterless hand cleaner on hand to remove the varnish from my hands.

13. I have a drying rack, which is a small board with thin brad-like nails that hold up to 15 eggs. Some people use this for melting the wax off in the oven. I like the quicker "hands-on" method of holding my completed egg over a small Bunsen burner or small hand propane torch. Just be careful not to burn your fingers.

14. One can buy an egg lathe to hold the egg. I do not own one. I just hold the egg in my left hand and work the design with my right.

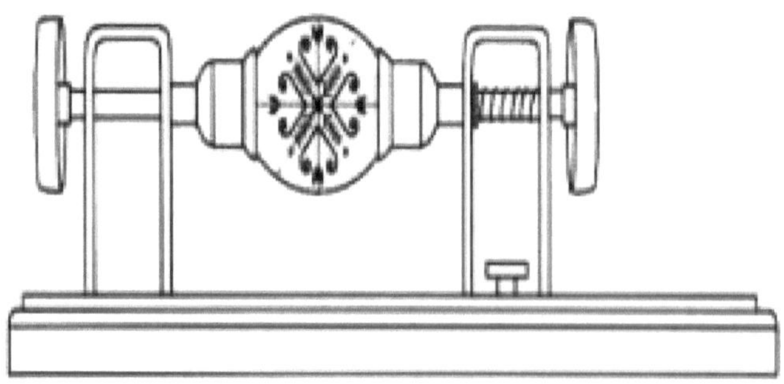

The following steps are basically easy.

Take your dry, clean egg and lay out your lines with light pencil marks. These will allow you to draw in your design.

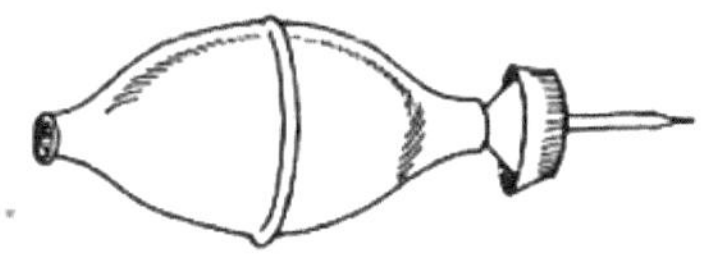

I do use an egg blower as blowing out the eggs gives me a tremendous head rush and that is something I do not need in my old age.

The next thing I do is to take my clean, dry egg and make the following grids so I can draw in my design. Just follow the diagrams in the order of 1 through 4.

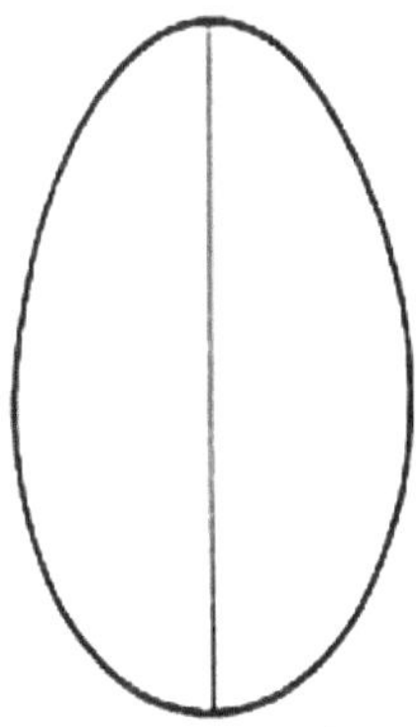

1. With pencil, lightly draw a line around the egg vertically, dividing the egg in half.

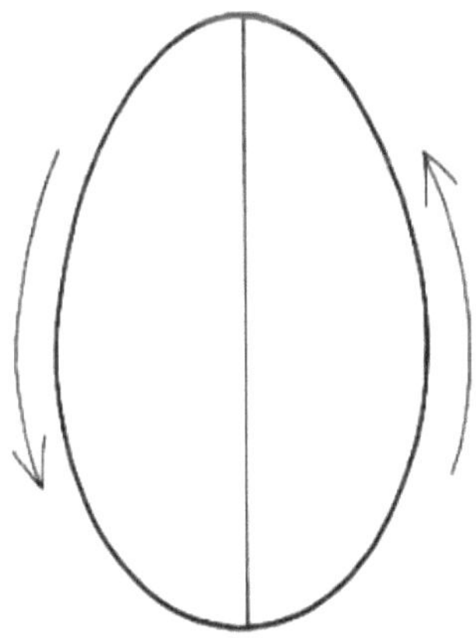

2. Now draw another line dividing the egg into fourths vertically.

Again these diagrams were given to me by my instructor to use again and again. You will find similar diagrams in about any book you buy on Pysanky or Ukrainian Egg Painting. I will share mine with you.

Remember to keep you pencil lines light!

<u>Don't be nervous about your lines.</u>

All it takes is practice. When you get to do many of them you will see yourself getting better and better. Soon you will have professionally looking eggs.

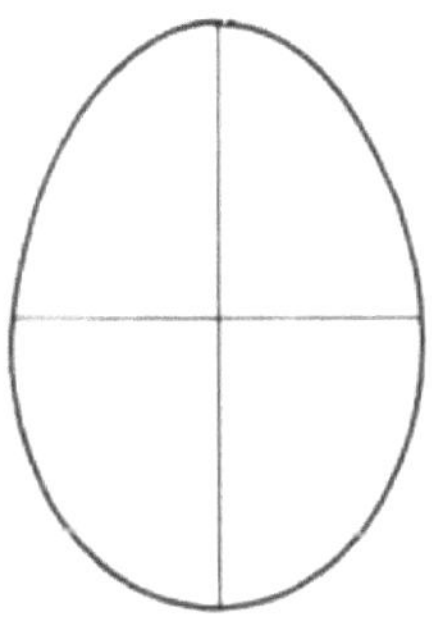

4. Divide the egg horizontally.

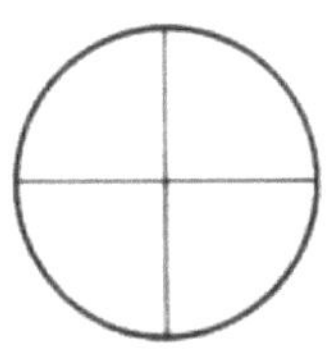

3. Top view of egg when step 2 is completed.

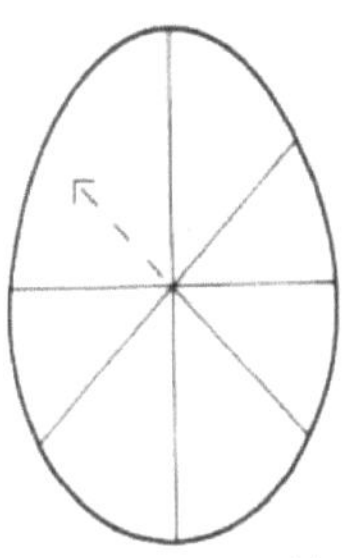

Start with basic division A, and then at the center point, draw lines dividing the egg into 16 equal parts. It should look the same on both sides.

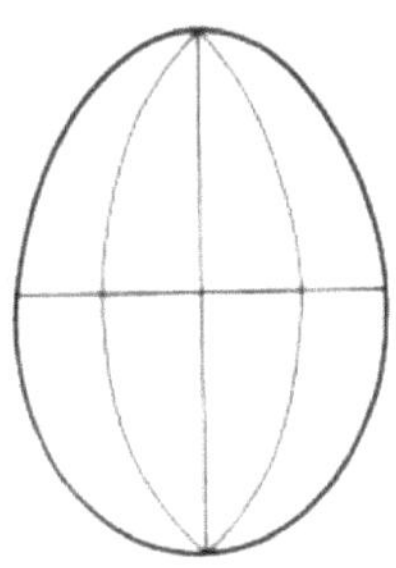

Start with basic division A, and then at the TOP of the egg, divide the egg into 16 sections with 2 additional vertical lines. The egg will look the same on both sides.

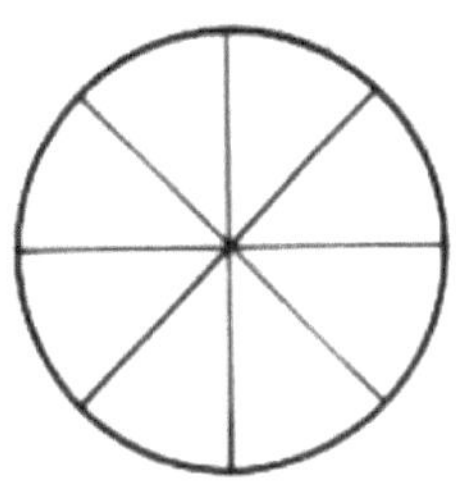

Top view of egg.

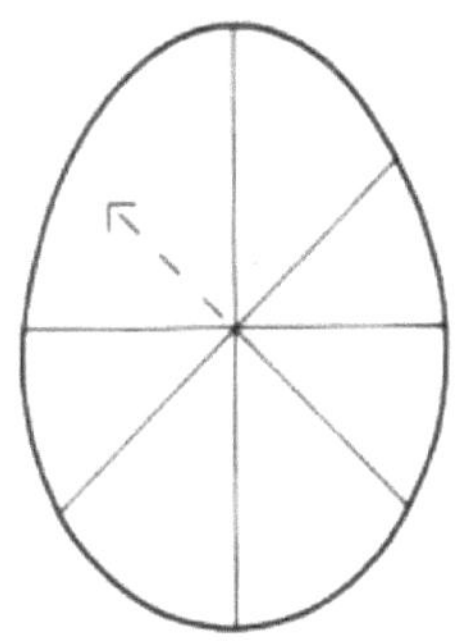

Start with basic division A, and then at the center point, draw lines dividing the egg into 16 equal parts. It should look the same on both sides.

This is basically a very easy thing to do. It just takes practice. As I said earlier I learned how to do this the in 1999 while wintering in Vero Beach FL. I took a $12.00 class at the public library and learned in one day!

The instructor said he had done a couple of thousand over the years. He supplied us with one egg and several photo copies of diagrams which I am including below.

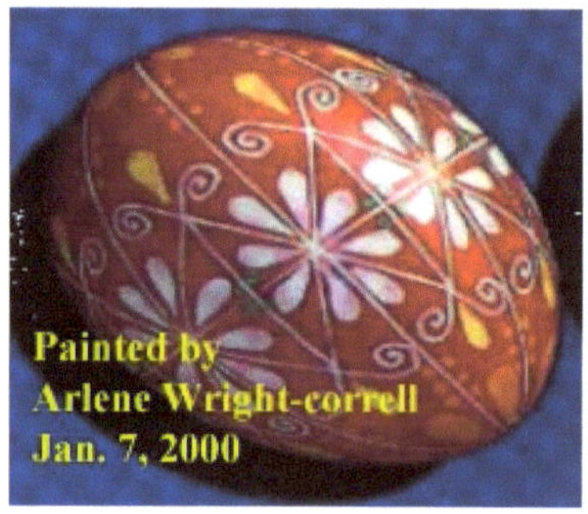

The first egg I did was not the greatest, but passable. Matter of fact I had the first one, but alas I never took a picture of it and then it got knocked off its stand in my art studio in 2007 and got crushed. However I practiced doing one a day for months. I bought so many eggs that winter it was amazing. After that I would do 1 or 2 a month. Many of them I put in the garbage pail. Many of them became good enough to give away as gifts after awhile. By the year 2000 they started to look like this.

Once you have your grid done, you can start sketching in your design and you can buy a book from the Ukrainian Gift Shop in Minneapolis, MN. Or go to your public library. This egg I made is called the Trypillian and the white was done with a medium and fine kistky covering the egg with beeswax. . One can change the ends of the kistky. The brick color was done with a heavy and medium kistky, covering the egg with beeswax and then dipping it into that color dye and black was put on for the final color. Then I held it over my small propane tank flame and let the wax melt so I could wipe it off as it melted, thus allowing the colors to show through. Then I blew the egg out and finally I sealed it with the varnish or polyurethane.

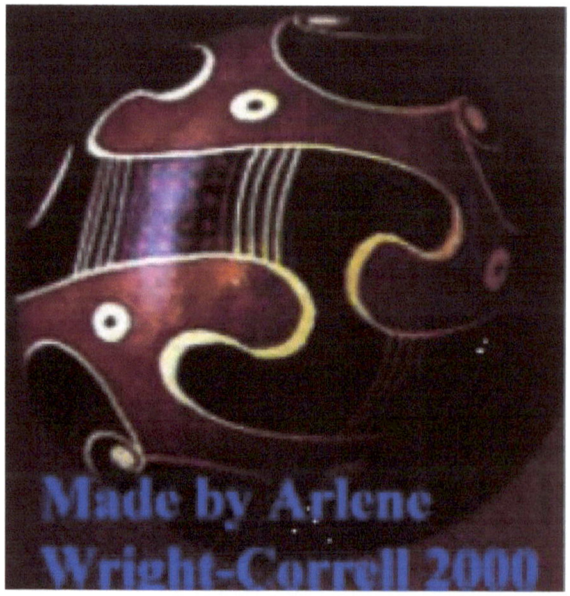

Trypillian eggs are from an ancient tribe of people that lived and thrived in the area of the Ukraine 6000 years ago. Pieces of their pottery were found near the little city of Trypillia only 40 miles from Kiev. The pottery designs adapt beautifully to the egg. Designs are of 3 colors. White, Black and Clay Red (brick). The designs are spirals and meanders which signify eternity and the cycle of life

Again as I have said, practice, practice, and practice.

Here are a few of the many eggs I did in the year 2000.

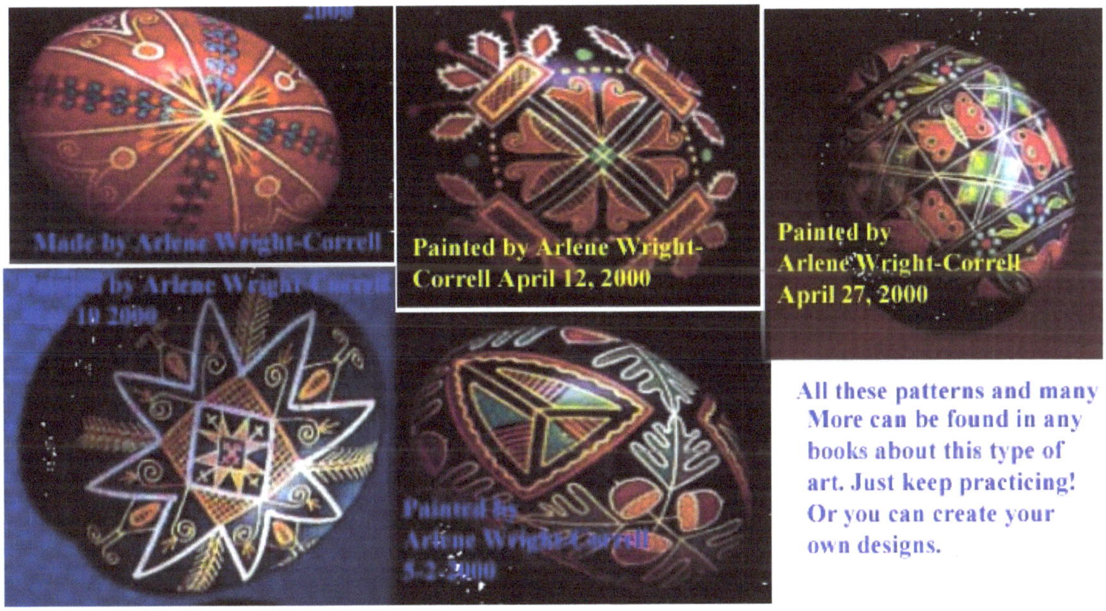

All these patterns and many More can be found in any books about this type of art. Just keep practicing! Or you can create your own designs.

In the beginning I was not very creative. I loved all the patterns in the books, so I just kept doing them over and over until I was quite good at reproducing them. The traditional designs are still my most favorite.

After awhile I discovered I could do my own designs and pictures. I found I was making Christmas ornaments with my grandchildren's names and the date on them. One year I made up some for all the tellers at my local bank. For my children I made up a dozen each and they loved them.

This chapter started out as a letter to Leonie and I hoped this helped Leonie. To you I say this is a satisfying hobby and can be done in the evening or anytime. It takes very little time except for the jars of dye. I have about 12 or 15 jars of colors now, so it is not something I can take with me. I have to do this at home.

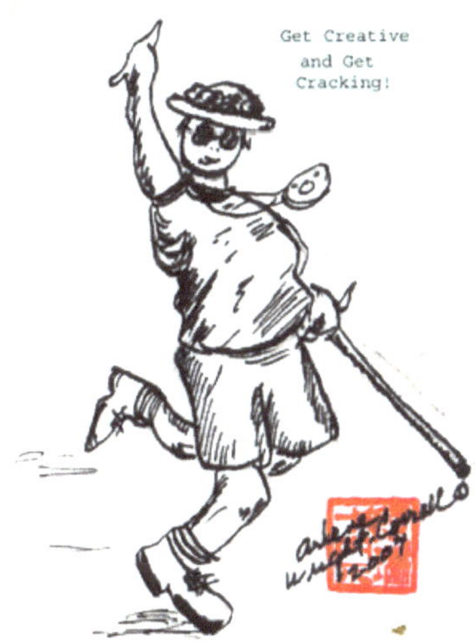

Just email me with any questions at askarlene@scrtc.com and if you are in the area, just stop in and say hello to us at Avalon Stained Glass School at 100 Dave Wintsch Rd., Munfordville, KY 42765.

Authors Note: Any of the images shown in this book are just the tools I use in my artwork. I am not endorsing any product or company. You basically can buy these from any art store.

Chapter 3

How to Work with Pastels

All pastel artwork by Arlene Wright-Correll

It wasn't until I was over 70 years old that I discovered the joy of working with pastels. I had picked up my paint brushes after 50 years of being a wife, homemaker, mother of 5 and running an incredible real estate career. After surviving a double mastectomy in 1992 and a stroke in 2000, I decided I needed to really relax myself and painting was it. Oils had always been my medium, then I discovered gouache watercolors and did mostly all my work in that medium for over 2 years. Now I was becoming familiar with pastels and it was really an interesting medium.

There are hard pastels, soft pastels, oil pastels, pastel pencils, and I included colored pencils and I have been having fun with them ever since. What exactly are pastels? I can remember as a kid using those big fat colored chalks and drawing on the sidewalks in Brooklyn outside our tenement building.

Roughly pastel began 250 years ago, although colored chalks have been used for thousands of years. Prehistoric cave paintings in southern France, Spain and South Africa show that man's early colored paintings used red, white, and ochre earth pigments, and burnt bone. Cave paintings in Lascaux, France, dating back more than 15,000 years, utilized charcoal and both wet and dry pigments to render huge animals on the vaulted ceilings. Presumably drawn and painted by torch-light, these early pictorials employ methods and materials similar to those used by pastel painters. Italian Renaissance Masters used red chalk to do architectural end engineering drawings. A work survives by Guido Reni 1575-1642, who produced the earliest paintings in a variety of colored chalks.

Most of us fail to realize that artists have been using these colored chalks for years. Art history shows that pastels center around France. Rosalba Carreira, born in Venice in 1675, became the first popular painter of the new medium. Recognized in Italy, she was the first to master the new medium, becoming the most fashionable pastelist in Paris. She used rubbing and blending, with a soft and delicate feeling and created beautiful portraits of French and Italian society women. After Carreira died, pastels were still popular in Europe. Our research shows that Jean Etienne Liotard, originally from Switzerland, did remarkably textured society portraits.

Maurice Quentin de La Tour 1704-1788, a great name in pastels, studied in Paris. His works were unpolished, not soft or delicate. His work showed competence, clarity, detail and freedom. Many pastelists emulated his frenzy of brilliant colors and textures. He gave pastel a new range and a rage that lasted four decades. Idol of thousands of Parisians, he inspired such painters as Watteau and Perroneau. Thanks to La Tour, pastel was equated with oil. Jean Baptiste Simeon Chardin 1699-1779, a highly studied and admired pastel painter, did subject matter of common kitchen utensils, bowls, cups, fruit, bread, rabbits and fish. In middle age, he gave in and painted oils. When he returned to pastels, he did an exquisite portrait of his wife. Pastel had no equal for freshness and spontaneity, and 75 years would pass before pastels would again rise in popularity.

From that period: Jean-Francois Millet, 1814-1875, lived only in the country, painting poor laborers and shepherds with flocks. He was also a superb oil painter, but his pastels, intimately described community life and brought the viewer into the pictures.

By the end of the 1860's, art was again changing...replaced by impressionism. Edouard Manet, 1832-1883, like many other artists of any era, battled public opinion, opposed the academy and worked with free strokes and loose handling. His full figures, devoid of background were considered radical, but a sign post to point the way for the new painters. In a year he accepted the new doctrine of light and air being developed by Monet, Pissarro and others. Of the original 30 members, Camille Pissarro 1830-1903, and Alfred Sisley 1839-1899 chose to paint only with this discipline of early impressionism. Cezanne boldly advanced, while recognition gradually declined for the others.

Renoir temporarily abandoned impressionism only later to return to it combining discipline with color, light and atmosphere in such paintings as "Les Canotiers". The hallmarks of this pastel period were aggressive strokes and colors. They were thinly applied to approximate cool atmospheric colors and emulate the transparency and sparkle of light. Edgar Degas 1834-1917 remains the most important pastel painter we can study. He greatly advanced pastel's total range of effects. He was fascinated by the camera, and cropping effects. He studied Japanese woodcuts by masters Hokasai and Hiroshigek and used flattened compositions, asymmetry and bright colors. Working to make his colors luminescent, he experimented with crosshatching, paints and pastel; he combined pastel with every medium, and surfaces of paper, cardboard and canvas. He mixed pastels with gouache and watercolor, and steamed them to soften pigments. With brushes, he manipulated colors and mediums, dipping pastels into prepared solutions and fixing each of the layers. He popularized the use and advanced the knowledge of fixatives. He drew and painted at the same time, constructing pictures, and enhancing illustration. Finally blindness ended his work in 1892. Degas pushed the envelope of pastel usage. Because of him, pastel was no longer considered a pale, pallid medium.

Other pastel visionaries were soon to follow. Odilon Radon, a contemporary of Degas, whose work was labeled post-impressionism, painted his subtle textures and strokes. His subject matter was personal visions, fantasies, dreams and figures. His beautiful floral works, mostly imagined, are his enduring legacy.

Ruth Henshaw 1772-1830, a primitive portrait artist from Massachusetts, created dramatic effects as she drew, using light from a candle to produce a silhouette accented by a simple pencil line.

The first American who could compete with the proficient Europeans, studied in Europe. James McNeil Whistler, of Massachusetts, attended classes at The Imperial Academy of Fine arts in Russia. Upon his father's death, he returned to America and went to West Point. When he was expelled, he left America, never to return again. Although he studied in Paris, his manners and temperament were strictly American.

Whistler was too interested in artistic problems to flatter his sitters; he was not a good colorist or draftsman. After he won his suit against art critic, John Ruskin, he was financially ruined. The city of Venice hired him to do a series of etchings. He meandered around the city with pastel while doing his commissions of etchings. He did 50 wonderful pastels. Whistler and his mother were well known. Other important pastelists of the period around 1898 were The American Ten, a group founded by J. Aldan Weir, John Twachtman, William Merritt Chase, Ernest Lawson and Child Hassam. Some consider that the Americans never reached prominence because they lacked daring, and failed to experiment. They tended more to the academic and illustrative and less to the explorative in their art. Childe Hassam, 1859-1935 stayed in Paris several times. He was most noted for flag motifs and local scenes of New York City.

Mary Cassatt, more European than American went to see La Tour's work. Associated with impressionists, she exhibited with them for the first time. She was an excellent draftswoman, doing inspired pastel portraits of mothers and children. She repeatedly used the same models, seeking a feeling of intimacy. Much admired, she created rounded forms with straight strokes. As she promoted the impressionists in the USA, counseling the Havermeyer family on art purchases of paintings for public and private galleries, it was clear that Impressionism had found its best friend and promoter.

Today, we have places that encourage painters in pastel and a whole roster of famous men and women who work in the medium. Among the organizations that have launched the "new Renaissance of Pastel" are The Pastel Society of America in New York City, the many important regional/national pastel societies such as The Pastel Society of the West Coast, The Degas Pastel Society, The Pastel Society of the Southeast, Pastel Society of the Southwest, the Pastel Society of North Florida, The Pastel Society of the Northwest, and The Pastel Society of Oregon. Other factors, publishers and organizations are The International Association of Pastel Societies, the proliferation of websites such as APOW, the manufacture of new lines of pastel, coverage in The Artist's Magazine and American Artist, and the publication of fine pastel books by North Light/ F&W Publications, Watson-Guptill and Rockport Publishers. Finally, with the proliferation of pastel, has come its monetary and cultural acceptance. It's the most permanent of all the mediums in existence. Its intrinsic beauty is without peer.

Yet after all this pastels still seem to be the “step child” of the art world. One usually cannot enter them into art contests unless there is a pastel section or it is a pastel art contest. A fledgling artist has to find a pastel society in hopes of being able to seek out a mentor or other pastelists. In my part of the world which is Kentucky, there does not seem to be an established pastel society.

Dry stick, Conté crayon, oil pastel and pencil pastels now form an aesthetic and technical bridge between drawing and painting. Originally employed by artists to work out compositional and color problems in preparation to painting with oil, the use of pastels evolved into a unique painting medium. Made from precipitated chalk, dry pigments and a binder (traditionally Gum tragacanth derived from Asian legume plants), modern pastels have been in constant use since the Renaissance.

Precipitated chalk, the essential constituent of pastels, is produced from geologically ancient soft sedentary limestone containing the shells of billions of dead marine protozoan. The limestone is finely ground in water and allowed to settle. The water is poured off and the resulting powdered paste is left to dry. Tonal ranges are created from various amounts of pigment blended with chalk paste.

Pastel is pure pigment, the same pigment used in making all fine art paints. All top quality pastel brands are permanent when applied to conservation ground and properly framed. Pastel that has not been sprayed with fixative contains no liquid binder that may cause other media to darken, yellow, crack or blister with time. Pastels from the 16th century exist today as fresh as the day they were painted.

The pure, powdered pigment, is ground into a paste with a small amount of gum binder then rolled into sticks. The infinite variety of colors in pastel, range from soft and subtle to strong and brilliant. The word pastel, in this case, does not refer to "pale colors" as it is commonly used in cosmetic and fashion venues.

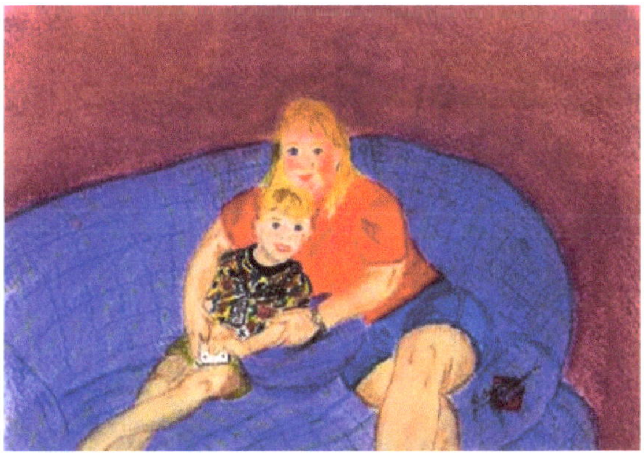

An artwork is created by stroking the sticks of dry pigment across an abrasive ground, embedding the color in the "tooth" of the paper, sandboard, canvas etc. If the ground is completely covered with pastel, the work is considered a pastel painting; such as the work on the left

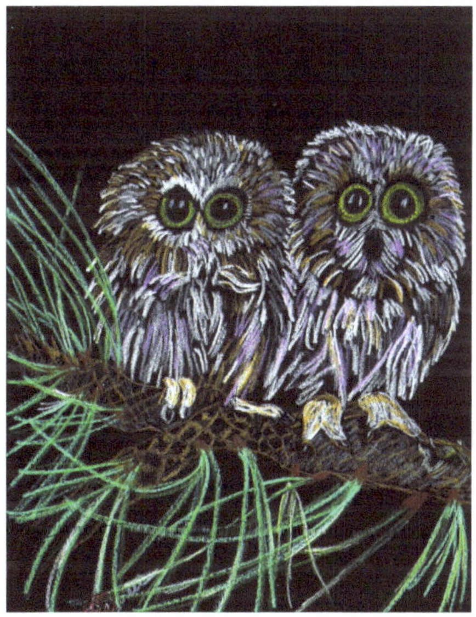

titled, " **Mom and Me"**. A work with much of the ground left exposed is termed a pastel sketch or drawing such as the work below on the right, titled, **"Whoos Who?"**. The painting on the left was sprayed with a fixative such as Krylon matte finish during the layering and a final coat at the finish. The pastel sketch on the right only received a coat of Krylon when it was completed.

Pastel is sometimes combined with watercolor, gouache, acrylic, charcoal or pencil in a mixed-media painting, but it is not compatible with oil paint. Pastel paintings reflect light like a prism. No other medium has the same color power.

Hard pastels have a higher portion of binder and less pigment, producing a sharp drawing material that is useful for fine details. These can be used with other pastels for drawing outlines and adding accents. However the colors are less brilliant than with, say, soft pastels. Semi-hard pastels such as the ones on the right have some brillant colors.

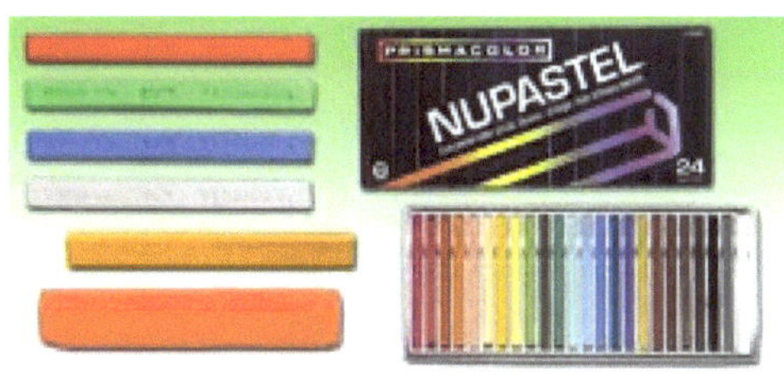

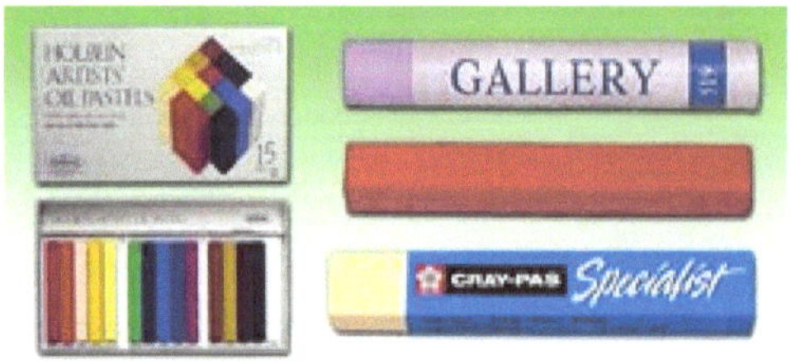

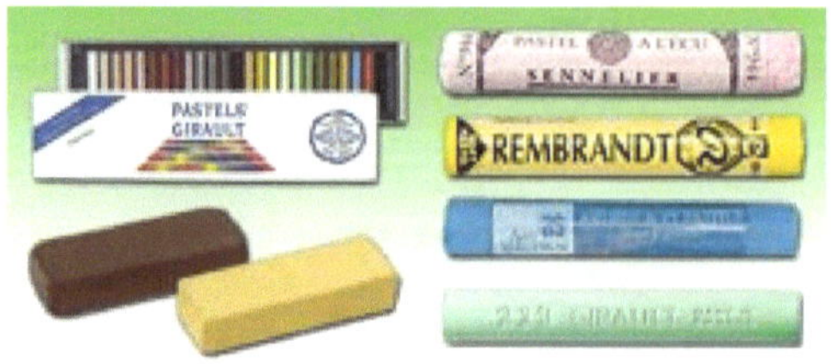

Oil pastels have a soft, buttery consistency and intense colors. They are slightly more difficult to blend than soft pastels, but do not require a fixative. The pastel painting of **"The Leopard"** was done in oil pastels. Though you cannot see it in this photo, I used a stylus to draw in the bark on the trees and the "etch" in the lines of the fur thus giving it depth. Since oil pastels have tendency to smudge so I gave it a final spray with Krylon fixative.

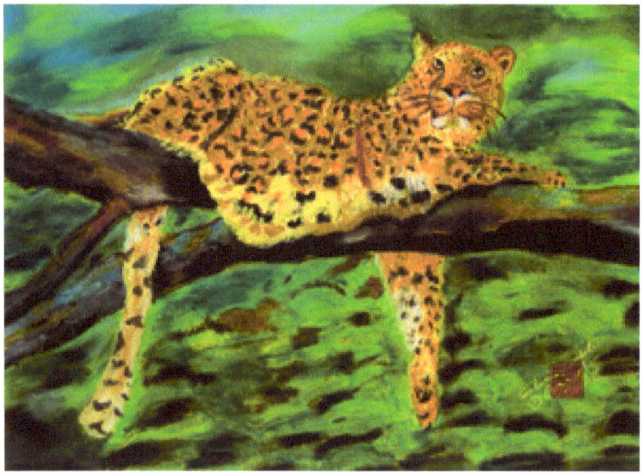

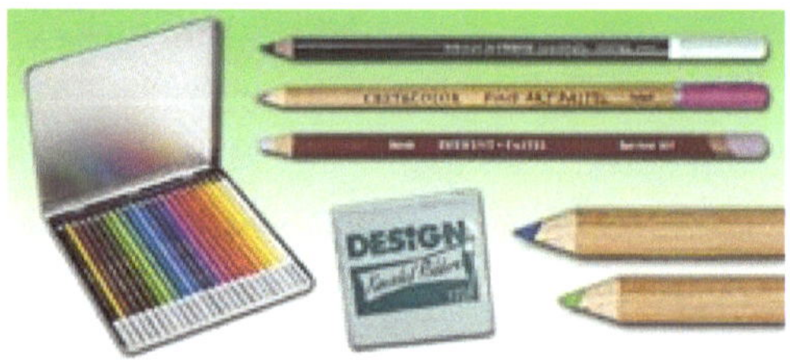

Pastel pencils are pencils with a pastel lead. They are useful for adding fine details. I find them quite a help in sketching, especially if you buy the eraseable ones.

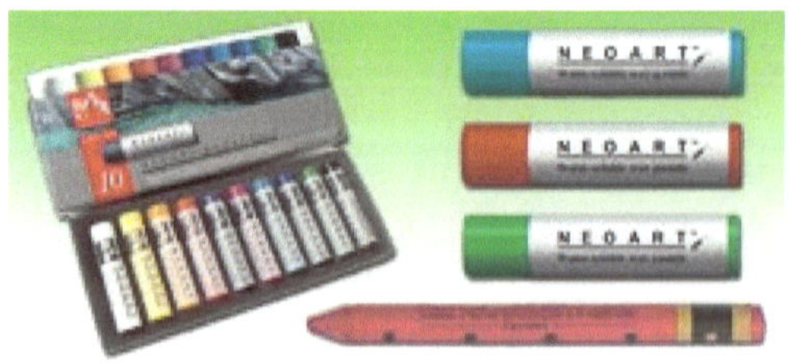

Soft pastels as shown on the left is the most widely used form of pastel. The sticks have a higher portion of pigment and less binder, resulting in brighter colors. The drawing can be readily smudged and blended, but it results in a higher proportion of dust. Drawings made with soft pastels require a fixative to prevent smudging.

Here is a pastel sketch titled **"The Lighthouse at Dusk"** done in soft pastels.

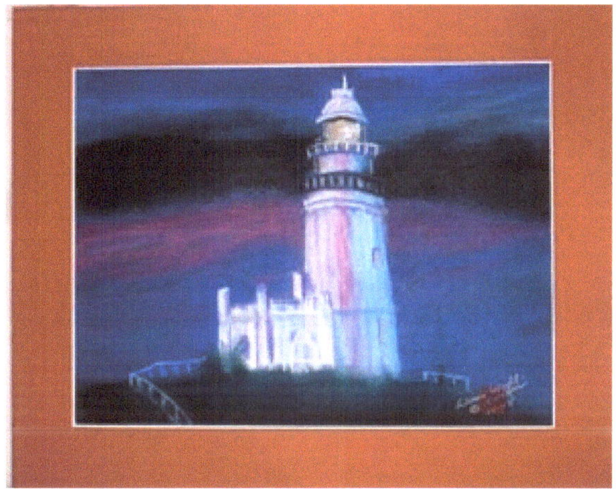

Water-soluble pastels are similar to soft pastels, but contain a water-soluble component. This allows the colors to be thinned out using a water wash. These I have just discovered and they come in a crayon type form. I had about $10.00 in Staples coupons the other day when I saw these and used the coupons to indulge myself in a small pack of basic colors. I am looking forward to experimenting with them.

I, like some artists, protect my finished pieces by spraying them with a fixative. In all cases, the pastel drawing or painting must be framed under glass to further protect it from smudging, environmental hazards, humidity, and so on. Drawings in a book of art paper can be protected by separating the pages using *laid* paper.

Pastels can be applied on a surface with some *tooth* (usually consisting of finely ground pumice or marble dust) which holds the pastel color in place. This avoids or minimizes the need for applying fixative which tends to darken and dull colors. I have just discovered these in the past few months and They are a delight to work with. I particularly like these papers by Art Spectrum. They come in cool tones or warm tones and with my Hobby Lobby coupon that week I was able to buy a pack of each for the price of one pack.

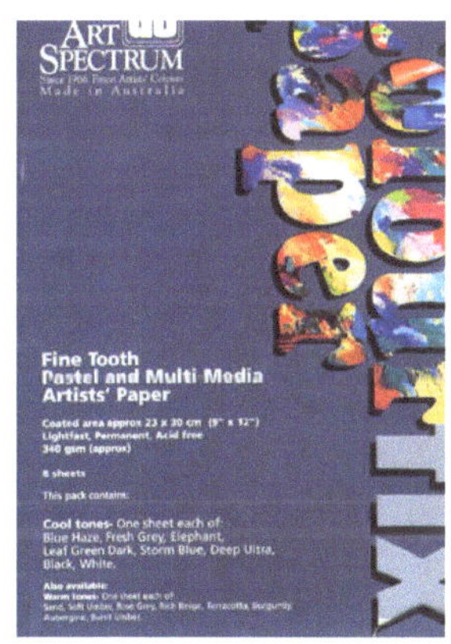

I enjoy trying new things and learning something new everyday.

Pastels have that quality.

I get a coupon every week from Hobby Lobby and just recently they had one for 50% off any of their art pads. I was able to buy about $300.00 worth of all types of paper for $150.00 which is just about my yearly art paper budget at this time of my life and was able to indulge myself in a great variety of paper. One might seriously consider getting on their mailing list. They send a flyer every week through the email. Just watch for the really good specials.

When I first decided to start dabbling seriously in pastels I was amazed at the prices of them regardless of whether they are hard, soft or whatever. A complete set of oil pastels can cost you about $400.00! I have to be very frugal with my spendable dollars in my old age. I find one can get very good values on line at Jerry's Artarama which are usually half price of most other sellers. Once I find something I want, I write down all the info including the prices and then go to eBay. I have been able to bid or buy on basically everything I wanted to get started and to get them anywhere from 1/3 to ½ less than Jerry's Artarama great prices. That may be worth the effort for you before you buy.

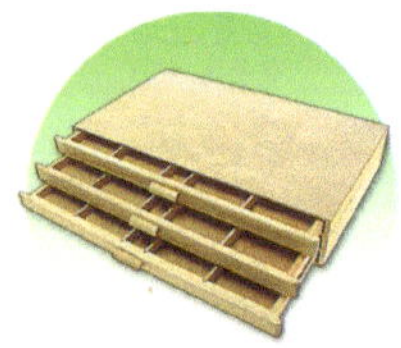

I was able to obtain oil, hard & soft pastels in landscape colors and portrait colors at very good prices from eBay sellers. At Jerry's Artarama I was able to buy 2 very nice sets of drawers they had on sale for the price of one in my local area. I show you a picture of them on the left. I was able to find a spot in my studio where I could put them one on top of the other, thus giving me 6 drawers. With a permanent marker I labeled the sections oil pastels, portrait hard, portrait soft, landscape hard, landscape soft and now have easy access next to my work space. So one just has to shop.

When I work with Oil pastels I find I can work at my slightly slanted art board I keep on my desk in my studio. When I work with soft pastels, I find I must work with my paper pinned or clipped to a large upright board at my french easel. These type of pastels create a lot of residue that has to be brush off constantly and I find it easier to have it fall straight down into a tray. I also find that I can add the fixative easier this way.

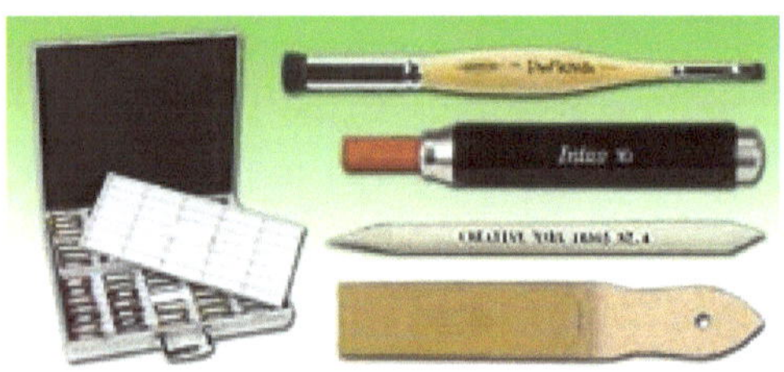

I don't use my hand or fingers with the oil pastels. I use pastel accessories such as you see on the right. The sandpaper stick I use to keep a fine point on my pastel pencils since the pencil sharpener seems to eat them up. I have never used a pastel holder.

When working with the soft, hard or semi-hard pastels I find myself using a series of pastel brushes or blender such as these. I enjoy working with the blending stumps & tortillions which can be shaped on the sandpaper stick pad.

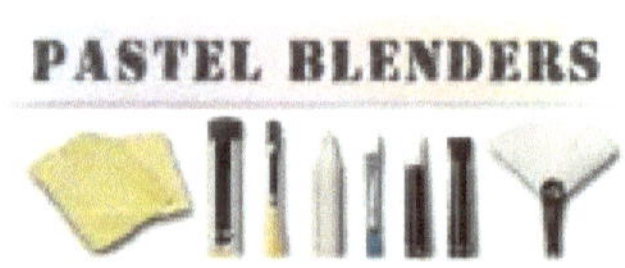

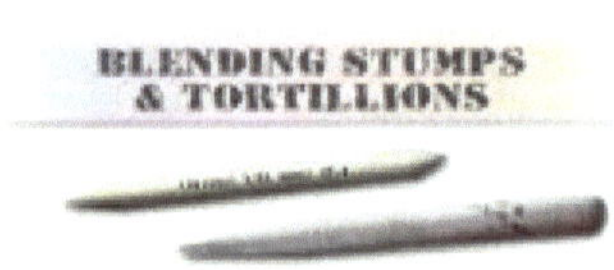

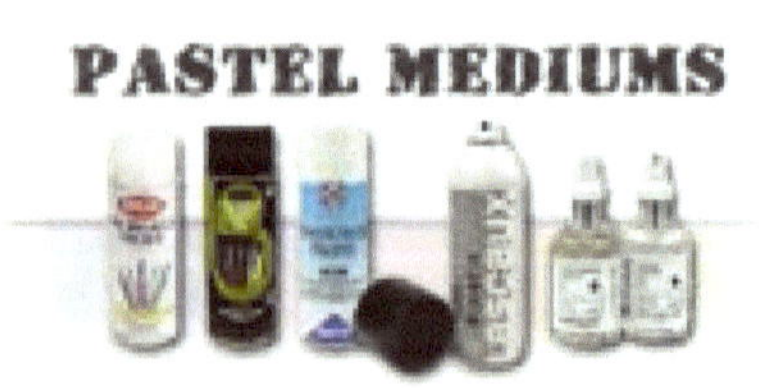

As I said many of us use some sort of fixative or medium and here are a few of them.

My own particular style, when working with oil pastels is to work from the back to the front of the painting. When I work with soft pastels, I usually work the same way, but may work from the top to the bottom of the painting, depending on the subject. This is something you will have to develop for yourself. Your own style or method.

If you have allergies you may want to use a face mask or even candy maker gloves. They are soft cotton. I wash mine right on my hands immediately when done and rinse the same, remove, wring out and hang them over the door handle of my oven where they air dry quite quickly.

Hopefully all this information will help you in your artistic search and perhaps cause you to try this medium if you have never used it before.

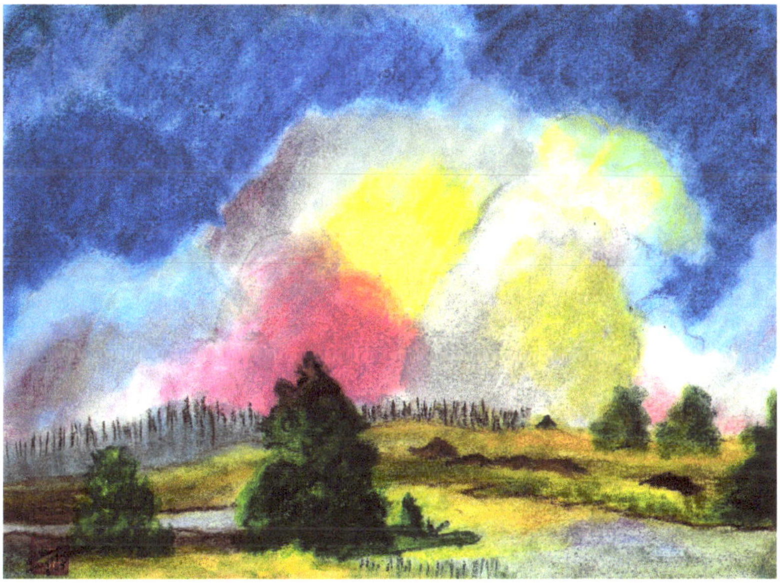

Just keep experimenting with it. Remember to draw, paint or sketch what you know. Your kitchen objects, your garden, whatever turns you on. Forget about all the nomenclature that gets attached to art. Just start and enjoy yourself.

It is so relaxing. It is a great hobby. It is something to keep your interest. There are never any mistakes, nor failures, just keep experimenting such as I did in the above painting titled, **"The Coming Storm".**

When I started doing my art again after a 50 year hiatius, I never dreamed I would sell any of my work. It is amazing. Sometimes I will do something that I think is totally terrible and someone snaps it up. Others I think are really good, just hang in my studio unsold. So who knows? "Beauty is in the eye of the beholder" as the saying goes. Just paint for yourself!

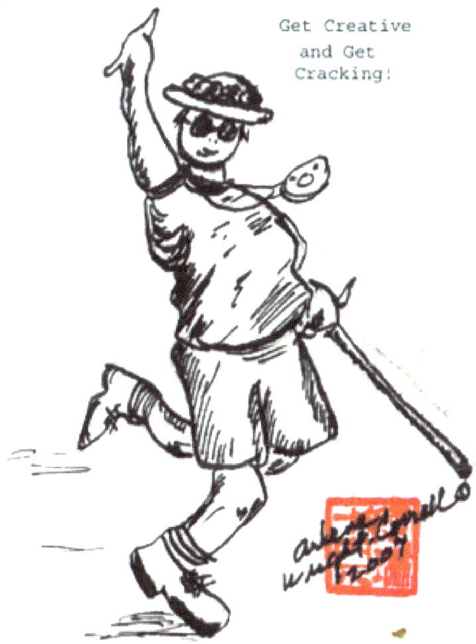

Authors Note: Any of the equipment or tool images shown in this book are just the tools I use in my artwork. I am not endorsing any product or company. You basically can buy these from any art store.

Chapter 4

How to Get Started in Acrylics

All paintings by Arlene Wright-Correll

Painting is basically simple and painting in acrylics helps to simplify the process even more.

Acrylic is a unique medium because it is very inexpensive and very easy to use. One only needs water for mixing, applying and cleaning up.

Many people choose acrylics to work with because they are allergic to solvents or the chemicals in oil paints.

Years ago there were only a few basic colors in acrylics and acrylic painting was considered the step child of the art world. Today it boggles the mind just read through an acrylic paint catalog.

Acrylics dry so fast it is basically only a matter of minutes and one can use it on a variety of surfaces from canvas board to glass to basically anything.

Once one learns a few simple techniques one can create paintings similar to oils and even watercolors.

Acrylics can be thinned to transparency or used directly from the tube like oil paints.

Acrylics dry durable and one can be worry free of it cracking or chipping over a time.

Here is the basic supply list one would need to start.

I suggest the following nine basic colors for your first palette.

Alizarin Crimson
Burnt Sienna
Cadmium Red Light
Cadmium Yellow Light
Cerulean Blue
Raw Sienna
Raw Umber
Titanium White
Ultramarine Blue

When one wants to develop the transparent technique I suggest the following 8 basic colors for your palette.

Burnt Sienna
Cadmium Red Medium
Cadmium Yellow Light
Mars Black
Phthalo Blue
Violet
Yellow Ochre Light

To get started there are a few supplies one needs to be able to get right into painting.

Small pointed round brush
1/8" round brush
¼" round brush
3/8" round brush
½" flat brush
1" flat brush
1-1/2" fan brush
Brush holder/tub for water
Palette knife, broad
Palette knife, narrow
Plastic Palette (with an airtight lid)
Support (for your painting surface) such as an easel or a slanted table.

Here is a list of optional supplies that one might want to add.

Acrylic Gesso
Gloss Medium
Gel Medium
Liquid Mask
Matt Medium
Non-flexible ruler (for a straight edge)
Retarder medium
Rubber Cement Thinner
Rubber Cement pick-up (eraser)
Spray Bottle
Tools for scratching and scoring

Your painting surface

As I said acrylics can be used on almost anything, including cotton or linen canvas, canvas board, watercolor paper or acid free matte board. You can paint even paint on wood, glass or metal.

What does some of these terms mean?

Acrylic gesso is used for sealing and protecting fabric and wood. Acrylics can be applied to unprimed canvas, but the gesso provides a smooth surface and a consistent degree of absorption of your paint.

Gloss Medium extends the paint and leaves a shiny surface when the colors dry. When you use a small amount of medium it makes it easier to move the paint. When you use a large amount of medium it will make your colors transparent.

Matte Medium will extend the paint and will reduce the glare when colors dry. When you use a small amount of matte medium it also will make it easier to move the paint and when you use a large amount it not only makes your colors transparent it gives you the ability to use them for glazes. **Think Thin When Thinking Glazes**
If you want transparent glazes, these should be built up in thin layers; a heavy layer will produce a glossy surface.

Retarding Medium is an additive for acrylic paints that slows down your drying time and makes the blending of colors easier.

Liquid Mask is used when you want to leave a surface free of paint. This will dry up and can be rubbed off later on. It is usually called "Fisket". I use an old brush to this or the cheapest brush I can find. Matter of fact there are some "Fisket" or masking tools one can buy that are fairly cheap.

Washing-up Liquid with Masking Fluid
masking fluid can be used with acrylics washes, as well as watercolors. Once masking fluid has dried in a brush, it's nearly impossible to remove. Dipping a brush into some washing-up liquid first makes it easier to wash masking fluid out of a brush. I find I just keep a small jar of water handy when I use this and just keep dipping the old brush into the water constantly because the fisket or liquid mask dries really fast and will do the same thing to the brush you are using.

Palette Tips:
Stay away from wooden palettes. Always choose a good surface to mix your paints such as plastic, Plexiglas™ or even a glass palette. One can use paper palettes; however remember they tend to make colors dry faster. A good airtight cover for your palette will preserve your unused paints.

Pump Bottle Tips:

It is best to have a pump spray bottle that will deliver a fine mist of water to keep your paints moist both on the painting and on your palette. Stay away from spray bottles that squirt as they will cause drips and runs on your painting.

I find that if you have city water you will have chlorine in your water. So use your city water, but first put it in an open quart jar and let it sit for about a half hour to let the chlorine gas escape and then pour it into your spray bottle.

Acrylic paint should never be used over oil painted surface. You can use an acrylic under –painting for oil paint.
Always use plastic or wooden tools for scratching or scoring. Never use metal tools as they can leave marks and create tears in paper and even canvas surfaces.

Keep a piece of paper towel or cloth next to your water jar and get into the habit of wiping your brushes on it after you rinse them.

Blending Acrylic Paints
because acrylics dry rapidly, you need to work fast if you wish to blend colors. If you're working on paper, dampening the paper will increase your working time.

Hard Edges
Masking tape can be put onto and removed from dried acrylic paint without damaging an existing layer. If you are painting on paper, then you must use a special artist masking tape so when it is removed it will not tear your paper. Use your hard ruler to draw your line for your masking tape. I like to use a T-Square to lay it out. This makes it easy to produce a hard or sharp edge. Make sure the edges of the tape are stuck down firmly and don't paint too thickly on the edges, otherwise you won't get a clean line when you lift it.

Always clean your brushes immediately with clean water because once acrylic paint dries on your brush it is permanent and can not be removed. Paint left on your palette will also become permanent when dried. Dried paint can be scraped off a glass palette with a razor blade. Be Careful working with razor blades.

An extra tip: Using Acrylic Paint as Glue for Collage
provided it's used fairly thickly and the item to be stuck isn't too heavy, acrylic paint will work as glue in a collage.

Now that you are set with this basic information you can proceed with your painting.

Can't think of a subject? Try arranging some simple items such as vegetables or fruits and try to copy them.

Don't think you can draw them? Find a simple picture you like and get a piece of graphite copy paper and put that between your canvas board and picture and trace it.

Many artists can paint, but they cannot draw and they use many techniques such as this type of tracing or grid drawing out a picture or even transposing it with a photo transposing piece of equipment.

Let your mind run free. Just paint colors. Your first painting will not be a masterpiece and maybe your 100th one will not be either.

Paint for the joy of painting and relaxing. Paint to relieve stress. Paint to express yourself and feel the flow of your feelings.

Don't worry about what others think or will say. Just start.
Angela Monet said, "Those who danced were thought to be quite insane by those who could not hear the music."

Here are five simple pictures I have done and you can copy them by just tracing them first with tracing paper and then putting a piece of artist graphite paper on your canvas, then laying your tracing paper on top of that and redrawing over your tracing thus ending up with your drawing on your canvas. Adirondack Barn

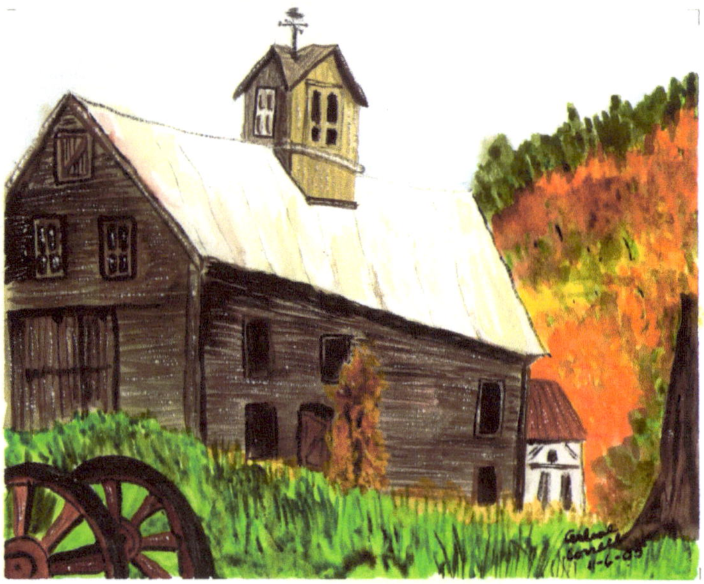

Start with a small canvas or better still a small 5 x 7 canvas board. You can usually by them in packs of 3 for about $2.95 in such stores as Hobby Lobby. Remember if you have a computer, you can go to their website www.hobbylobby.com and sign up for their flyer and it will be in your email every Saturday and it will usually have a 40% off coupon for any one thing you want to buy in the store that is not on sale that week. I save a lot of money that way. You can find the location for your store. Just remember they are not open on Sunday.

You can also find similar deals at Michaels. I do find that Hobby Lobby has better sales, more consistent sales and a greater variety. Yet if you happen to be in either store, remember to go to their clearance sections. I find the greatest bargains.

Also if you have a large discount coupon for something you want that week and it is not in stock, they will usually give you a rain check for it, just make sure you have them write that you can use that week's 40% off coupon and make sure you save the coupon with the rain check.

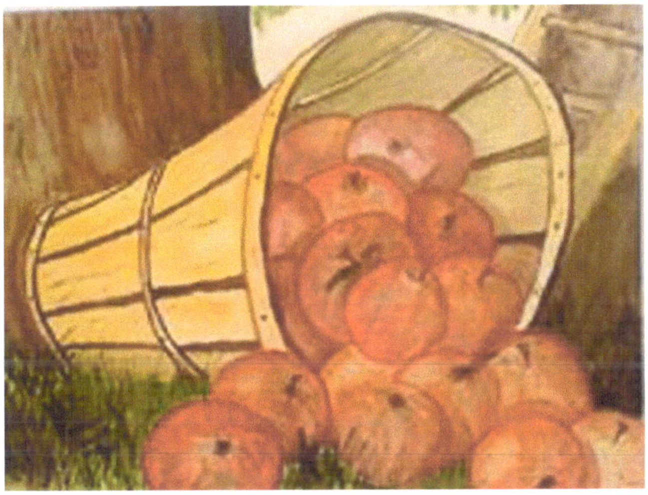

"Apple Picking Time©"

Here is another subject you may want to try in your practices. "3 Apples"

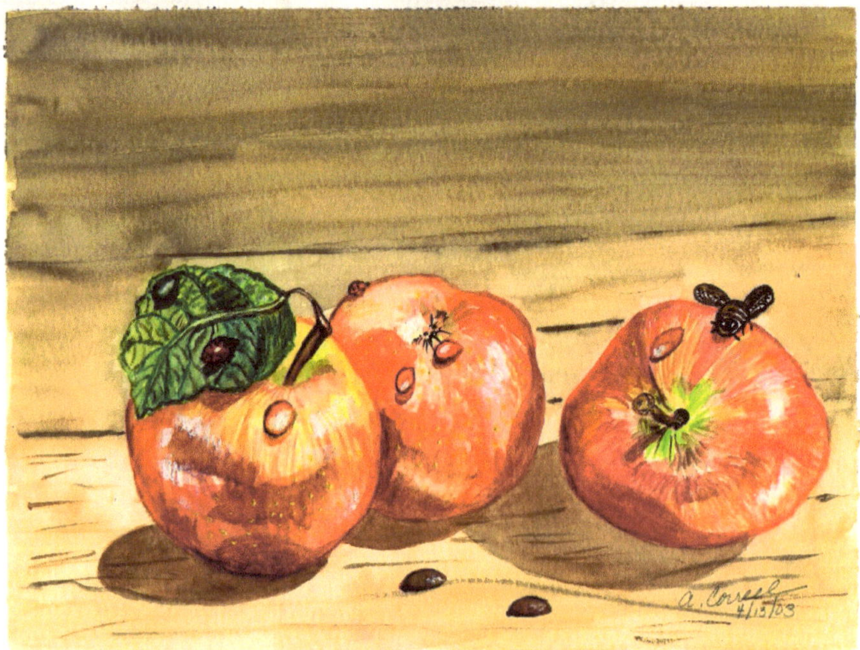

"Kentucky Morning Mist©"

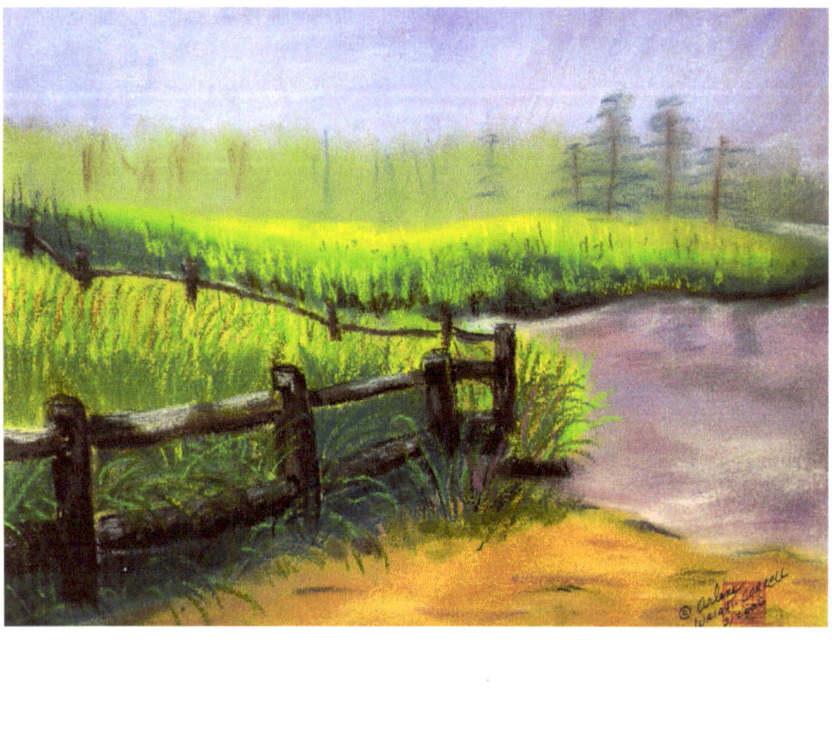

"Crack Rider©"

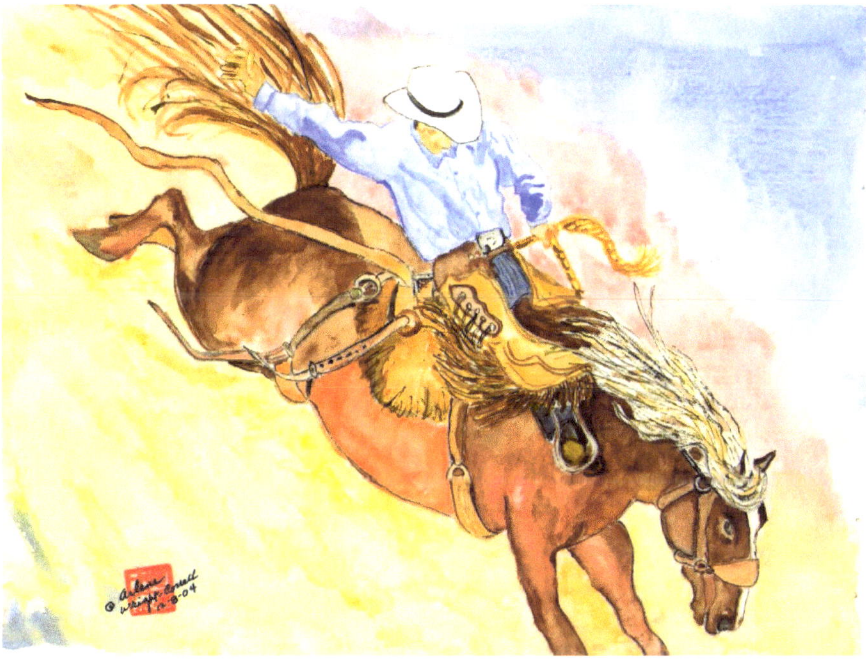

Remember that this is supposed to be fun, something to relax you and ease your stress.

Something to get your creative juices flowing again and don't be afraid of making mistakes because some of the mistakes can be scraped off, painted over or just become a really great painting.

Just remember that Van Gogh never sold a painting during his life time and that Renoir sold a painting now and then for as low as 15 cents!

You may never want to sell a painting and you may never want to show them to anyone. However, should you wish to try your hand at any of these arts or crafts, and then try it.

What do you really have to lose? Think about all the fun you will have and remember to surround yourself with people who are better than you in whatever field you would like to excel in. These will become your mentors. Never work with small minds.

Believe me when I say that every one of these people started at the bottom. It is nothing more than practice, drill and rehearse!

Chapter 5

How to Get Started in Oil Painting

Painting is basically simple and the first and most important thing is that you need to learn the language of oil paint. You see, oil paint has its own laws. It is wet, it is done with brushes, and it is not what you have been used to for your whole life. In other words, it is not drawing. The materials used to make oil paintings carry some rules with it that you must know.

Next you must learn the process of oil painting from beginning to end knowing what to do step by step. We must realize that unless we know the basic we can become lost or confused again while painting your paintings. It's just like anything else you know a procedure to. I think you would agree that a surgeon knows the procedure to perform an operation. A carpenter knows the procedure for building a cabinet. You need to know a procedure for making a painting of whatever you feel like.

When you begin your painting--Do you draw on the canvas or panel right away? Do you draw on paper first? Do you draw with pencil on the canvas or panel? The answer is you can do all of these things. You should be able to choose the method that best suits you.

You will need to know all the steps to painting your pictures to completion. This involves things like...

* under painting
* glazing
* knowing about composition
* tone values

Here is the basic supply list one would need to start.

Brushes You should have many brushes so that not to lose time washing them while working. Take a new brush for every new mix. Use round kolinsky brushes, #1 to #10. To cover larger surfaces, you will need a few #20 to #35 brushes. For final strokes PRIPLAVLENIYE (final blending) you will need a few very soft round and flat average size squirrel brushes. Brushes should be treated very carefully. After every session they should be washed in turpentine and after that in warm water with soap.

I suggest the following oil painting supplies:

Grumtine*/art grade turpentine

Oil Paints

Titanium White
Burnt Sienna

Burnt Umber
Cadmium Yellow Medium
Cadmium Yellow Deep (or Cadmium Orange)
Cadmium Yellow Light or pale
Grumbacher* Red
Alizarin Crimson
Cerulean Blue
Cobalt Blue
French Ultramarine Blue
Sap Green
Veridian Green
Yellow Ochre
Raw Sienna
Raw Umber
Payne's Gray

Place your pallet in the above chromatic order. If you keep your paints in a specific order on your pallet you will not waste time hunting for the right color or accidentally mix the wrong colors.

A good tip is to start out with small tubes of paint and then as you find which ones you are using more of then buy those colors in larger tubes.

Painting Medium"
This is used to thin your paint to a smooth consistency. There are various ones on the market today. Some add shine or gloss, some dry faster; make sure you read the labels carefully.

To get started there are a few supplies one needs to be able to get right into painting.

Sable Small pointed round brush
1/8" round brush
¼" round brush
3/8" round brush
White Bristle flat-medium & 1½" flat brush
1" flat brush
1-1/2" fan brush
Brush holder/tub for turpentine or cleaner
Palette knife, broad
Palette knife, narrow
Plastic Palette (with an airtight lid)
Support (for your painting surface) such as an easel or a slanted table.
Bar of gentle soap for cleaning brushes
Paper towels

Palette Tips:

The true old time artists feel the palette must be made of hard dark wood, best of all, of pear. After work wash the palette with turpentine and scrape it with a razor. Before work wipe the palette with linseed oil. This is o.k., but feel free to use a plastic palette or even palette sheets on a pad.

Your painting surface

As I said oils can be used on almost anything, including cotton or linen canvas, canvas board, watercolor paper or acid free matte board. You can paint even paint on wood, glass or metal. In the old days the true artist said the canvas should be primed additionally a few more times and in conclusion it should be ground with fine sandpaper. After that the canvas should be scraped with a razor to remove the canvas texture till smooth dead surface similar to the egg's surface is achieved. Today the canvases can be purchased all set and ready to go to work on.

Now that you are set with this basic information you can proceed with your painting.

Can't think of a subject? Try arranging some simple items such as vegetables or fruits and try to copy them.

Don't think you can draw them? Find a simple picture you like and get a piece of graphite copy paper and put that between your canvas board and picture and trace it.

Many artists can paint, but they cannot draw and they use many techniques such as this type of tracing or grid drawing out a picture or even transposing it with a photo transposing piece of equipment.

Let your mind run free. Just paint colors. Your first painting will not be a masterpiece and maybe your 100th one will not be either.

Paint for the joy of painting and relaxing. Paint to relieve stress. Paint to express yourself and feel the flow of your feelings.

Don't worry about what others think or will say.

Just start.

Here is an example of painting like the Dutch Masters who used the 7 layers of paint. The artist Engr guaranteed to his clients this quality for 300 years.

<table>
<tr><td>The first step is making the drawing.</td><td>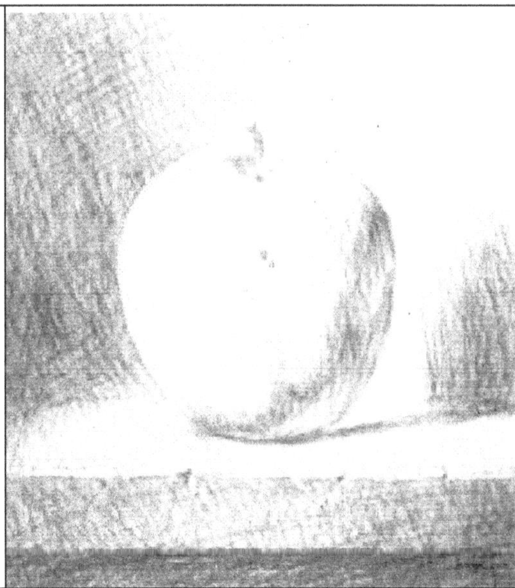</td></tr>
<tr><td>Next you transfer your drawing onto the canvas</td><td>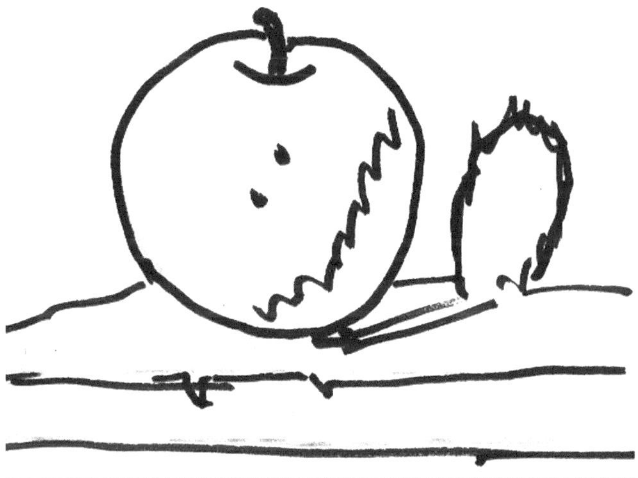</td></tr>
</table>

Step 1 is adding the first layer of paint	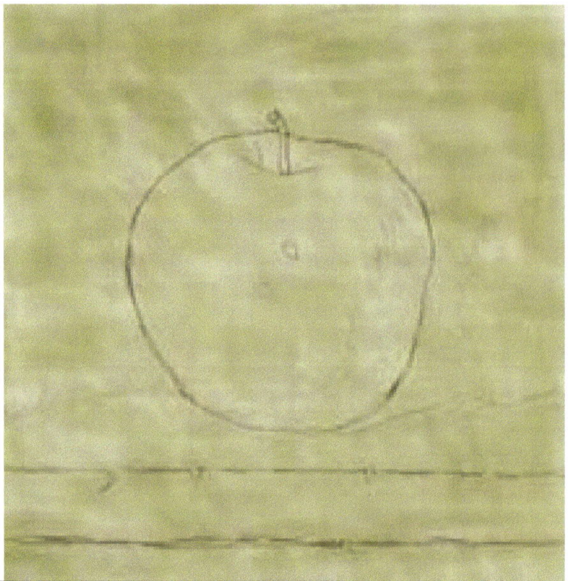
Step 2 is adding the shadow or the 2nd layer of paint	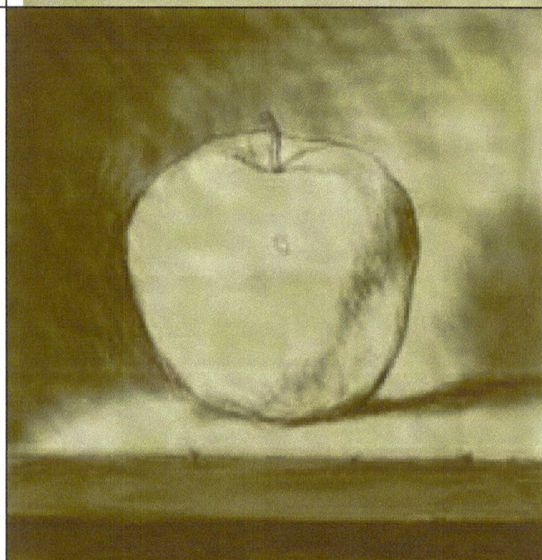
Step 3 is defining the shadow by adding the 3rd layer of paint	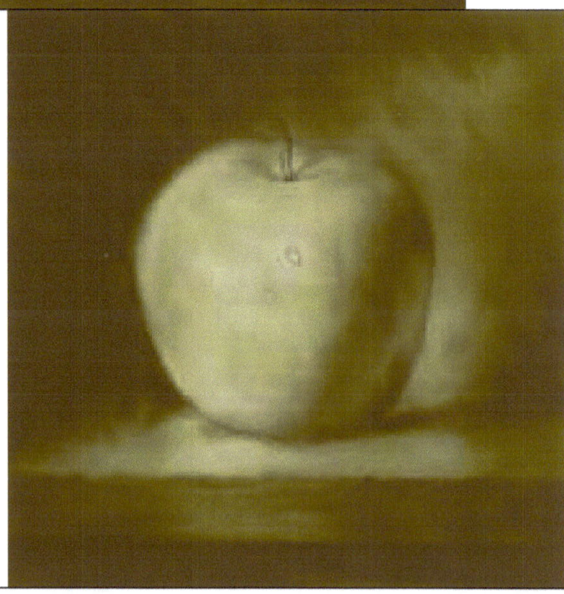

Step 4 is adding the dead layer or the 4th layer of paint.	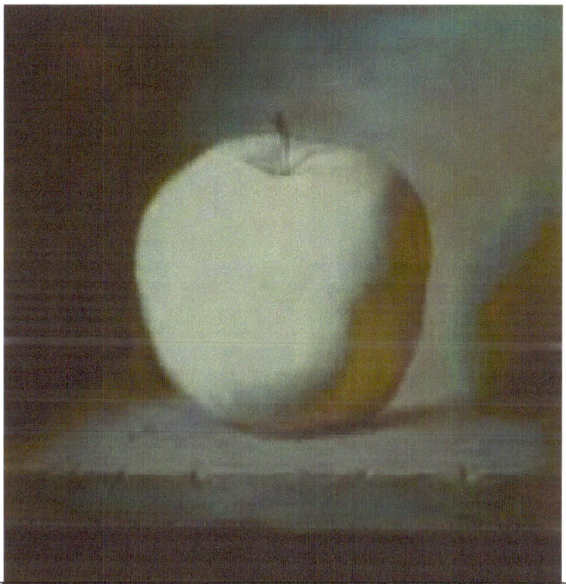
Step 5 is adding the 5th layer of paint	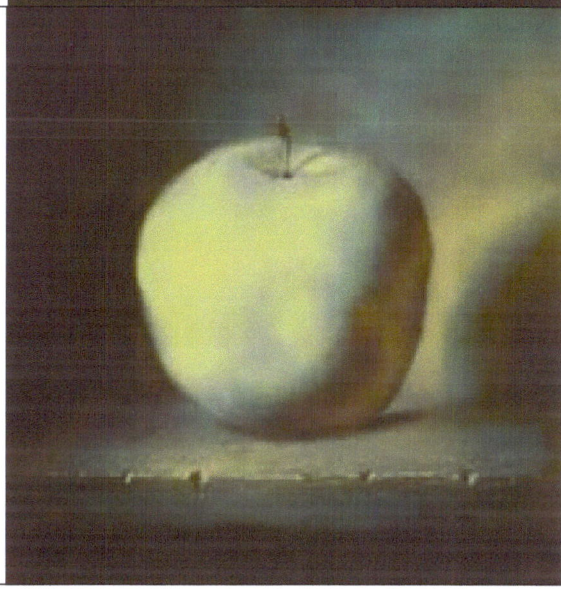

Step 6th is called going back to the body or adding the 6th layer of paint.	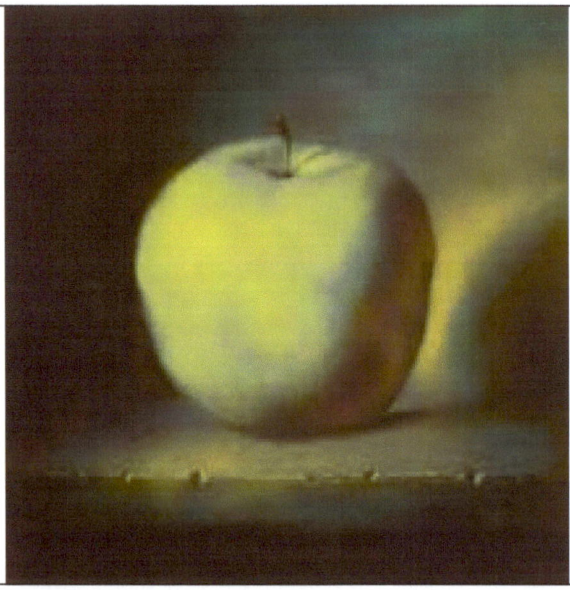
Step 7 is adding details in the 7the layer of paint.	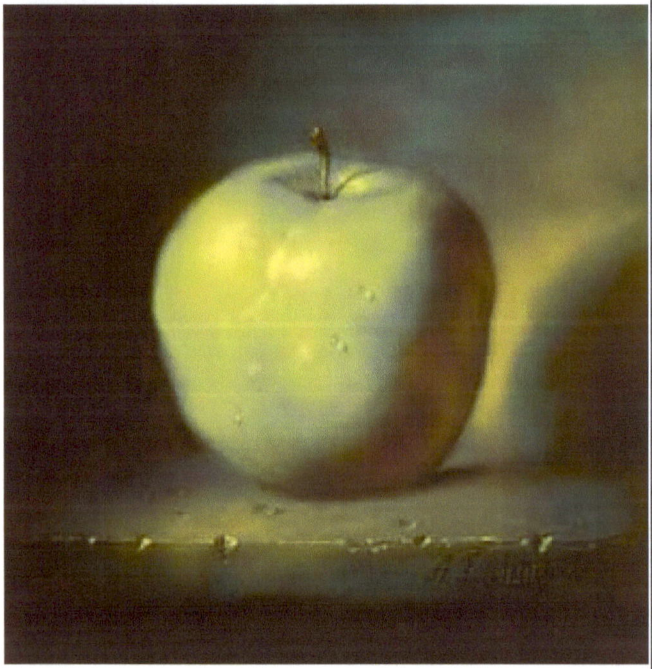

Here are some paintings I have done that you can copy for exercises in oil painting.

Oil painting is not for the impatient since it takes awhile for oil paints to dry and you must be able to have space to do them in.

Here is also a simple oil painting procedure.

1. Make thumbnail sketches of your subject to see how you would like it to be placed on your canvas.
2. Draw a grid on your sketch
3. Draw a grid on your canvas or on a piece of paper the size of your canvas and then you can transfer your larger drawing onto your canvas using graphite paper or artist transfer paper
4. When you transfer your drawing using graphite or artist paper use a ink pen or stylus to draw your transfer with.
5. Next paint the entire canvas with thinned oil paint in Ultramarine Blue or Burnt Umber.
6. Paint the entire canvas with a thin wash of oil paint. Paint each area approximately the right color and do not worry about the details since this thin wash is your color map to judge your color scheme and to provide a common adhesive layer to help the thicker paint adhere to the canvas and avoid cracking.
7. Begin painting the objects that are visually the furthest back like the sky or wall. Never paint an object that is in the front and the try to paint the background around it as it will always show. You will need to allow some drying time between layers of paint.

When you thin your paint use a painting medium or turpentine.

Always wash brushes first in turpentine and then with a mild bar of soap to remove the oils from the base of the bristles and then rise thoroughly. Stand your brushes in a jar with the bristles up to dry.

When the painting is completely dry to touch then and only then apply retouch varnish to protect the painting. After 6 months you can apply Damar or a good commercial varnish.

Always clean the painting before applying the final varnish. Dip a soft cloth in warm water with a little mild dish soap, wring out completely, and then carefully wipe down the surface of the painting. Rinse the same way and never allow the canvas to get wet.

Do not hang your paintings in direct sunlight or the colors will fade. Never hang an oil painting over an air conditioner or heat vent or the temperature variations will cause your paint to crack.

When framing a canvas never put a backing on a oil painting as the painting must "Breathe" from both sides so the thick paint will not mold.

"The Grand Canal, Venice, Italy©"

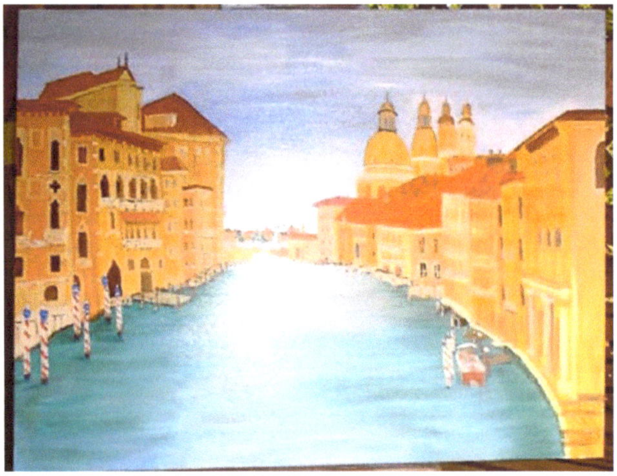

"Mediterranean Dry Dock©"

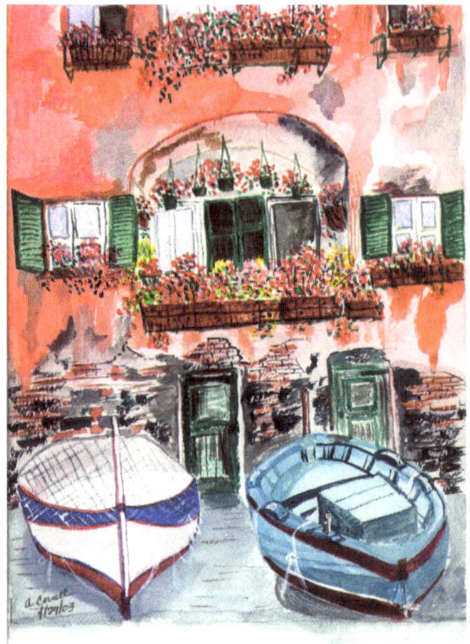

"Lavender Fields©"

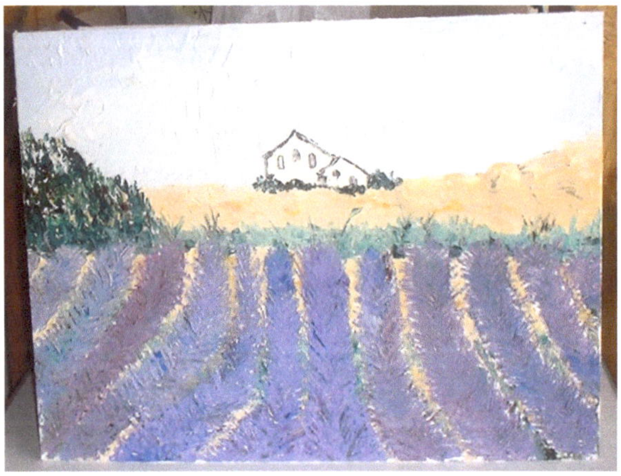

"The Tuscan Courtyard©"

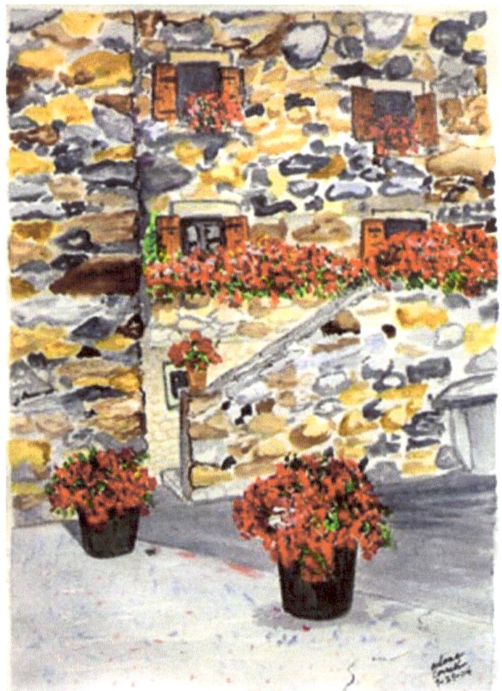

There is never a reason to not to try something. Who knows what you will put on paper. Feel free to copy every one of these paintings. Try your hand at copying anything. Develop a style. You do not need to develop my style or anyone else's.

Do remember that many budding artist' spend hours in a museum copying other famous artist's work just for the practice. If you don't have a museum in your area that allows that, then buy a book or a calendar and start copying some works. ***Get Creative and get cracking!***

Chapter 6

How to do Scratchbord Art

I first discovered scratchbord art by accident. It was at the clearance aisle in an art store. Here was a little kit that had the scratch pen missing. As a consumer I could not resist the bargain price and as an artist I could not hold back my curiosity and now I am an addict.

Scratchboard art or scraperboard art is a technique where drawings are scratched into ink painted over a thin layer of white clay which has been laid over poster board or another stiff paper. These boards are also called scratchboard or scraperboard after the technique.

Sometimes scratchboards are made with several layers of multi-colored clay, so the pressure exerted on the instrument used determines the color that is revealed. Using scratchboard is said to yield a highly detailed and textured piece of work far beyond that of traditional paintings.

In the 19th century cardboard was coated with chalk, but this quickly progressed to the use of India ink in parts of Europe which prevails to this day. Scratchboard became popular for its "finer" line appearance, and could be photographically reduced for reproduction easily without losing quality and it was used mainly for advertising and editorial illustrations until computers made that outmoded in the mid 1950's. Now it has made a comeback as an appealing art medium. More recently Claybord, a finer medium, has been created to provide easier and more detail works.

I like Claybord Black which is clay coated hardboard panel for scratchboard and it is coated with black India ink. Similar to traditional paper scratchboard, I like it because it is more durable and easier to scratch into for cleaner and crisper details and lines. Wherever I want to add dimension, I add colored India inks to the white areas and then scratched again for additional highlights and volume.

The nice thing about Claybord black is in the event I make a mistake I can just take some more India ink and cover my mistake, let it dry and begin again.

Using a sharp, angled blade, an outline is made on the surface of the scratchboard. Depending on my design and what I want to create several areas are often cleared out for layering with these colored India inks or even watercolors or acrylics. I then scratch off the layers one by one to create different shades of color that blend into and highlight certain parts of my image. When needed, I can retouch with more paint as necessary. This technique can yield an image that appears remarkably lifelike.

The charm of Claybord or scratch board is that the cleared portions of the board can be left blank for a stark black-and-white image that is offset with the various colors of India ink that I have applied. Various techniques such as hatching or stippling can be used to texture and detail the image further.

Scratchboard may be either all black or all white. Claybord often also come in tan, brown or light blue. When one uses the white scratchboard one will draw black areas onto it and then proceed to scratch into the black portions to create ones drawing. India ink is typically used for creating the black areas.

This is a stimulating and challenging art form which gives great finished works of art.

Start with the little kit which comes with the stylus and instructions and pattern. Then graduate to buying small packs of Claybord and some Claybord pattern books.

Here are the first ones I ever did.

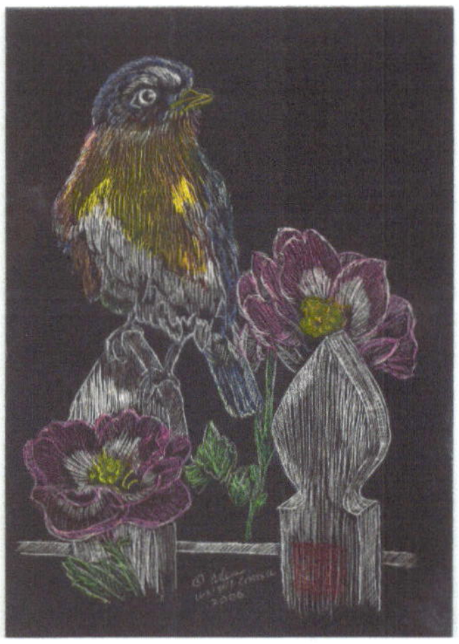

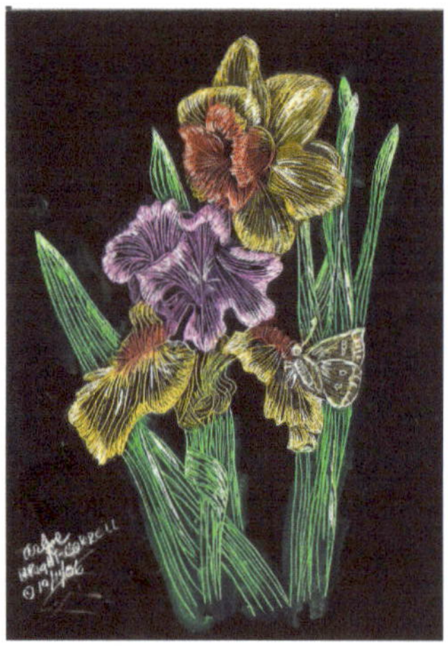

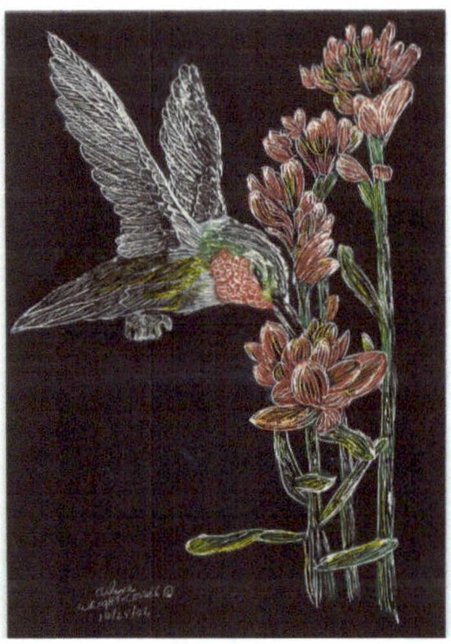

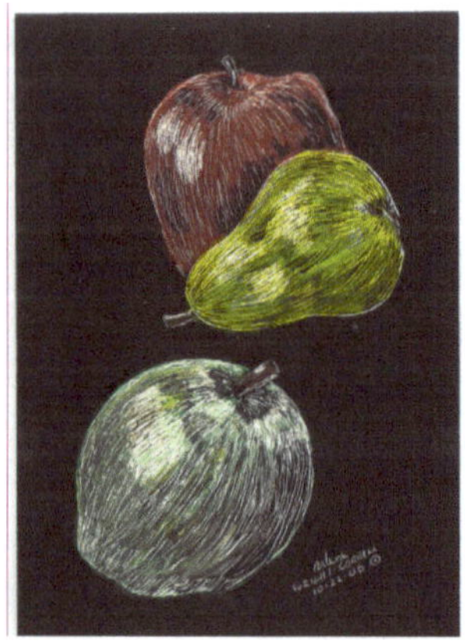

Then I did two more and I was hooked.

Next I found a pattern book called the "ABC's of Flowers" for Scratch Art or Claybord. Since I am a gardener I decided to try it. It took me 4 months to complete it. That is not every day, but 26 days out of 4 months because I was doing other things.

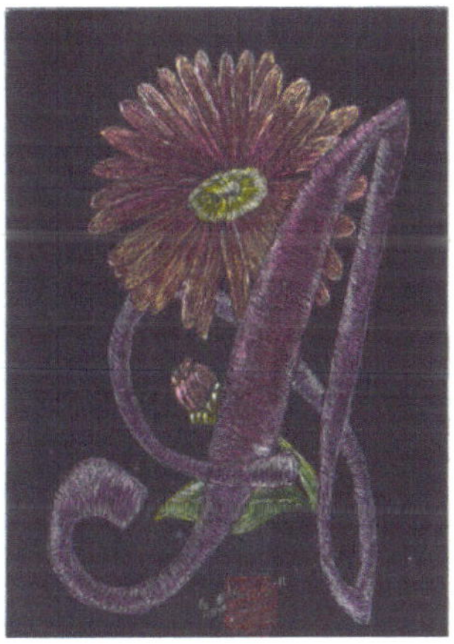

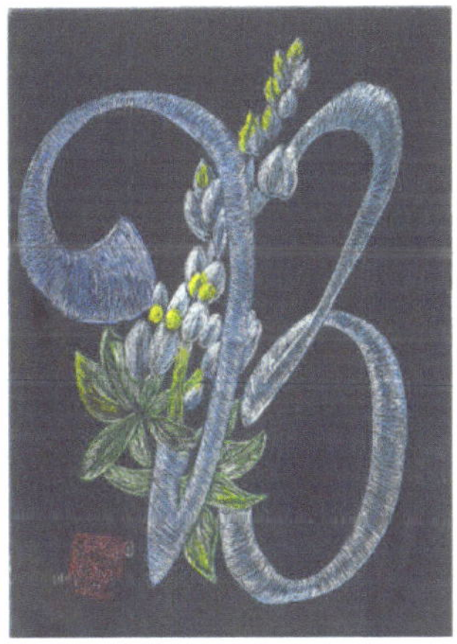

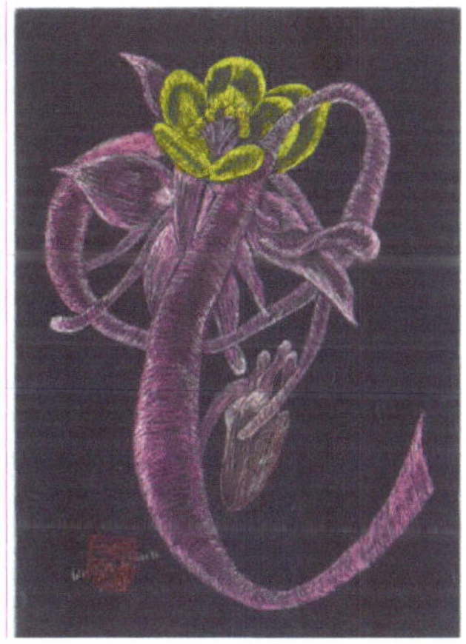

Etc, etc until done and here is the final piece of work I entered into The Women in the Arts show Bowling Green, KY in 2007 and my One Woman Exhibition in Glasgow, KY also in 2007 and the KY State Fair 2007. It now is displayed in the Glasgow Cultural Center Art Store waiting for a buyer. It is the size of a door.

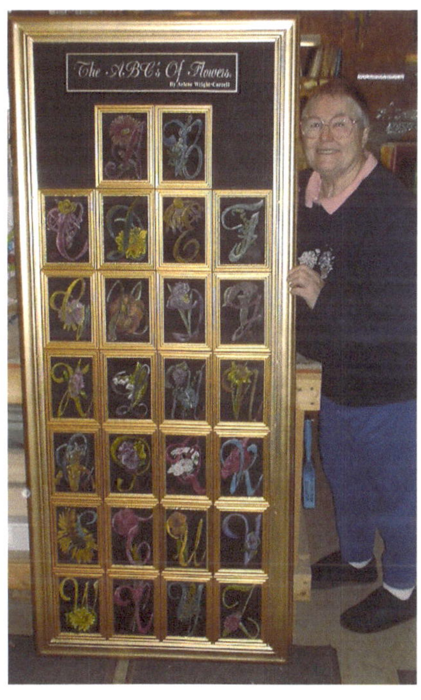

They could be broken down and sold individually as they have been mounted as removable. However, I hope someone buys it as it is.

Since then I have my copyrighted copies available as Giclee prints on www.imagekind.com and then type in Arlene Wright-Correll then click on all galleries and you will be able to click on one of the pictures that shows this type of work.

And you can get post cards and lovely note cards of each individual flower at
http://www.cafepress.com/arlene_correll

Now do your realize what you can do with your work as you expand your mind? Leave yourself open to all new creative experiences. Go to arts and crafts shows, sit in on local art groups, believe it or not they usually welcome all newcomers who are expressing interest in learning what they are doing.
Get creative and get cracking!

Chapter 7

How to Turn your Travels into a Sketch Book

If you like to travel and don't mind keeping a daily diary as you travel and if you have a camera, preferably a digital one, you can create a great traveling sketch book upon your return home. Here is an opportunity to really stretch and grow!

This can become a memorable piece of art work for you and your family. The paintings can be framed and displayed in your home, you can set it up on your website, and you can create post cards to send to friends and family members afterwards.

I discovered at the end of this work called **"The Spanish Sketch Book, or the 4 Amigos Go to Spain"** that I had basically become an "illustrator" and I had a grand piece of descriptive writing. For those of you who travel at a much slower pace and enjoy Plein Air Painting, you might not need a digital camera. If you travel with my brother, George, there is no such thing as a slower pace. Or if you travel on a tour bus, there is no such thing as a slower pace. Take your camera and paint later at home or in your studio.

Here is my illustrated diary to prove my point.

"The Spanish Sketch Book or the 4 Amigos Go to Spain"

All watercolor paintings by Arlene Wright-Correll

In our old age, for the past several years, Carl and I have taken holidays with my brother, George and his wife Barbara. We have been all over the world and the American Southwest with them. We have seen wonderful things and have had great times. Thus, each year, we (Carl and I) literally save our pennies for one big 2 week trip some place with them. George, though about 3 years past retirement, is still working and we plan everything around the vacation time he can get. We have done cruises, Europe, the Caribbean, the Mediterranean, the American Southwest and have gone in all different modes of travel, including renting

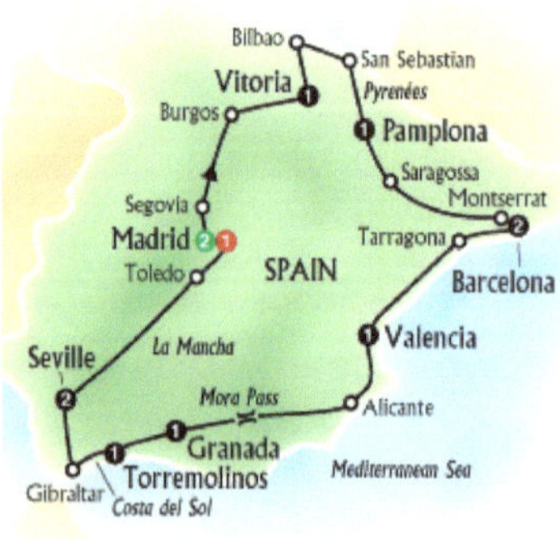

a big motor home for 16 days.

Carl and I have done day bus trips and I like them because Carl and I both get to sightsee when someone else drives as opposed to Carl driving while sightseeing and me never seeing anything because I have my eyes on the road. George and Barbara have done several extended Germany bus trips with their gang of friends who fill up an 80 passenger bus and literally have control of what they are doing, so they have good bus trip memories.

With that in mind, plus we are all getting long in the tooth, we four decided that we would avail ourselves of the offer at "Vacations to Go" and take a 14 day Spain Globus Bus Escorted Tour titled, "The Spanish Fiesta". Little did we know!

At this point, let me say that had it not been the 4 of us who make our own good time, we could not have endured this trip. We saw lots of wonderful things, but we were flying past the things we really would have stopped to see had we been driving. 250 to 300 miles a day and it was on the bus, off the bus, on the bus, off the bus. Plus the tour guide ticked me off about the 4th day, and ticked each of us off at various times, did not make for great relations.

Most days it was up by 6 am, luggage in the hall no later than 7 am, breakfast at 7 am, and on the bus at 8 am. Barbara is not a morning person! Nor is she a breakfast person! Both Barbara and I are diabetics so we have to eat at certain times and in Spain as in most of the Mediterranean countries, everything closes down from about 1 pm until 3 or 4 pm. Siesta! Also most restaurants do not serve dinner until 8, 9, or 10 pm. Plus Spanish people, including almost all of the 84 tourists on this bus trip, party all night because they have big naps in the afternoon. There were lots of people sleeping on the bus every afternoon. The 4 of us could not stay awake past 9 pm without great effort.

All and all, we had a great trip, but it was Carl and mine first extended bus trip and it will be our last. I think George and Barbara concur. Thus it was hard for me to write about this trip. Every time I started to think about it, I got irritated.... That is until August 27th, 2005 when I started to think about doing some paintings of the trip. I had recently done one about our visit to the Spanish Square in Seville as you will see later on and we were pleased with it. I decided to do a second one as a painting essay of our trip. The map above shows our route. We flew into Madrid, headed north, and looped around the coast and back through the middle again to return to Madrid in order to fly home.

Hence, the "**Spanish Sketch Book, or the 4 Amigos Go to Spain"** © is born! This will be a work in progress as I have no idea how long it will be to write this and paint what I remember. Along the way, as usual, I kept a diary about our days. This article contains some excepts from it.

6/15/05 Carl and I left for Louisville airport real early. We are real anxious for this trip and are looking forward to it. We left Louisville at 6 am, changed in Atlanta and met George at the Islip airport at 2 pm. He had the champagne chilling in the refrigerator! We arrived at George and Barbara's in Sayville, NY 2 days before the trip and we got to visit and get ready for the trip, plus go to all the great restaurants they have in their neighborhood, plus get to eat some great New York Pizza!

We had an opportunity to visit with our niece, Lorijean and her daughter Gialian. Gialian, who is 12 years old, had just received a lovely and elaborate community service award, signed and given to her by President George Bush. Three other signatures were also on it, including John Glenn and Bob Dole.

Barbara and I visited, George had to finish some work and Carl walked into the village of Sayville to window shop and to buy some goodies that we can not get in our area.
That evening George took us all to a lovely restaurant in Oakdale called Mama's and we had some fine Italian food.

6/16/05 This morning Barbara, Carl and I drove around the old parts of Long Island while George was finishing up his work. We found our old house in Bohemia which we sold in 1967 and it looked a lot different. The John Pearl Grade School is still functioning. Donald and Donna went to school there when they were 6 and 8 years old. We drove over to visit Barbara's 92 year old mother, Winnie. Her sister Judy was there also and we had not seen her since 1968. A pleasant surprise for me was a large oil painting I had done of a wooden bridge back about 1965. I had totally forgotten I had painted that. There it was on Winnie's wall in her living room where it has been ever since the day she acquired it. We went back and we treated dinner that night at a great Chinese restaurant in their area.

Day 1, Friday, June 17th, 2005
The next morning, George drove us all over our all growing up neighborhoods. What a lot of change and growth. I would never have recognized most of the places he showed me.
We enjoyed a nice New York Pizza for lunch and then headed out to JFK. We boarded our overnight flight out of JFK in New York at 6:15 pm. It was a long flight, especially for Barbara and me.

Day 2, Saturday, June 18th, 2005, we arrive in Milan, Italy at 7:55 am and have to make a mad dash to catch the 10 am connecting flight out to Spain. That seems like plenty of time. However, in Europe it is not and especially when the air line is Al Italia. Plus this airport makes O'Hare and Atlanta seem like a breeze!

Nothing is orderly. They do not board by sections or by row numbers, they just say, "boarding" and it is a mad dash with about 200 people or so, with their carry-on luggage, trying to board a plane!

We finally arrived in Madrid, Spain where we cooled our heels in the airport for almost 2 hours while a couple was trying to retrieve their luggage lost in Paris. George does not have the patience of a saint. Finally, both of us told the tour greeter to get us unto a bus and deal with the lost luggage couple separately. We four were beat on our feet! "Let them take a taxi to the hotel", says George. While waiting to get out of the airport we met Val and Verna from Australia, A Cuban couple from Michigan, Margo from Cambera, Australia. We finally arrived at the Hotel Aqura in Madrid.

We have side by side, but not adjourning rooms where we all get to take a nap before the orientation meeting reception that evening. All except George, who is our "scout" and checks out everything before we go to wherever we go. He let us know that there was a big Gay Rights demonstration in down town Madrid that evening. At dinner we met a young Cuban man who escaped from Castro's Cuba, also 4 ladies from California, of which 2 were originally from Guatemala 40 years ago.

The dinner was good and consisted of salad, chicken & ice cream cake for desert. Afterwards the 4 of us walked to a nice sidewalk café that George had found earlier and we sat with our beers, talked and people-watched. The weather is hot, but very dry. Madrid is growing and bustling. Lots of building going on and most people live in high rises which are being erected by the dozens, daily.

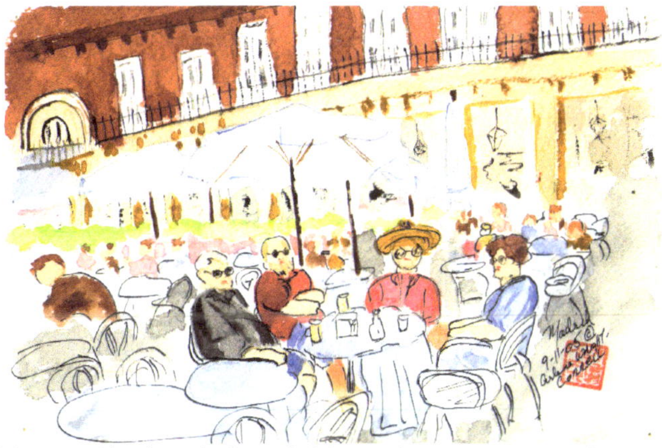

Day 3, Sunday, June 19th, 2005
We are up early, luggage out, and down for a hearty buffet breakfast at 7:30 am. The bus left at 8:30 to give us a tour of downtown Madrid and it's highlights such as Don Quixote Square, The Royal Palace which has 2800 rooms, Plaza de Isabella II, and the Real Mayor, just to mention a few. We also went to Puerta de Sol, Plaza de Espana with its monument to Cervantes, the Parliament, Cibeles Fountain, Elegant Calle Alcala, and Paseo de Castellana.

Madrid is the capital of Spain since 1562, is located on the geographic center of the Iberian Peninsula. Because of its central location and high altitude, the climate of Madrid is characterized by warm dry summers and cool winters. Madrid is a city of great monuments. Among its highlights is the medieval center dating back to the Habsburg Empire and the Prado Museum.

But Madrid is not just a cultural destination. It is also a lively metropolis with many pubs, cafes, discotheques and nightclubs open late into the night. One can get stuck in a traffic jam at four in the morning, and the people you meet are not necessarily going off to work.

In the afternoon we went to the Prado were we saw the works of *Velazquez, El Greco, Zurbarán, Murillo* and *Tizian*, as well works by masters of the *Flemish school*. It was a brilliant experience.
That late afternoon there was an optional tour to El Escorial and the Valley of the Fallen. However, we were pooped out by then.

Day 4, Monday June 20th, 2005.
"If it's Monday, it must be Segovia"

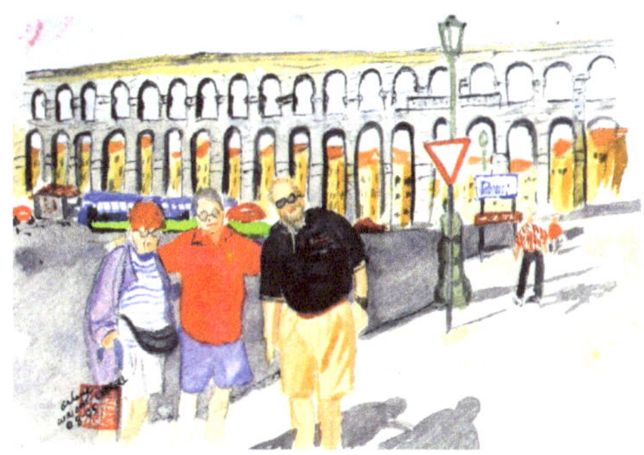

Segovia is Spain and Castile at its best - twisting alleyways, the highest concentration of Romanesque churches in all of Europe, pedestrian streets where no cars are allowed, the aroma of roast suckling pig around every corner - all surrounded by the city's medieval wall which itself is bordered by two rivers and an extensive green-belt park with miles of shaded walks.

Here we are, Barbara, Carl and George in front of the city's 2,000 year old Roman aqueduct cuts right through the center of town. Its symbol has served as the mintmark on all coins struck in Segovia for over 400 years. I am the picture taker and it was a hot day. Too hot to walk around and as usual we arrived at the time of day when everything was closing down for siestas. Only 53 miles separate Segovia from Madrid by road. The Navacerrada ski resort lies exactly halfway in between the two cities at more than 7,000 ft. elevation. Then it was back on the bus and on to Burgos.

Burgos served as one of the capitals of Castile (Castilla), the historic heart of Spain and was the birthplace of the Spanish 11th Century hero El Cid. The city's remarkable Gothic cathedral is a building of exceptional beauty, and one of the country's largest. It is here the tomb of 'El Cid' lies. The Old Quarter preserves Renaissance churches and palaces. The San Millan Suso and Yuso monasteries are also worth a visit while in Burgos. 15km east of Burgos there is a totally different attraction- the Atapuerta archeological site. It contains prehistoric tools and bones of the earliest humans in Europe, living some 800,000 years ago.

Burgos is a charming historical town. We walked around it. Again we were there during the siesta hours when most everything was closed. We really disliked this part of the Globus tour. There is a little park in the center with a bronze statue of a Shepard or saint and George sat on his lap since there was no room on the bench after Carl and Barbara were on it. I snapped the photo, but took artistic license and painted myself into the picture. "Taking a Rest in Burgos"

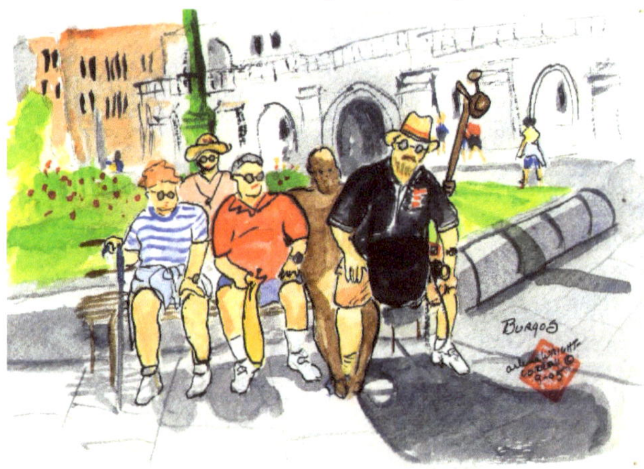

Back on the bus and on to Victoria. It was too modern for all of us. It rained hard right after we arrived, so we were unable to get into the old historic part of town.

Rincon de la Victoria is sometimes described by local residents as a "dormitory town". Situated just 12km east of Malaga, it makes a convenient base for those who work in the city but prefer sea breezes and beaches, and the relative tranquility of an overgrown fishing village. It is also a popular place for the Spanish to "veranear" (spend the summer months) and many families have their second home here. The municipality of Rincon includes the neighbor fishing village La Cala del Moral and the pretty inland village of Benagalbon.

Rapid expansion in the last five years or so, however, with apartment blocks springing up literally overnight, has meant that services are overstretched in July and August. The winter population of 26, 600 inhabitants almost triples during this period. The rest of the year, the town retains a laid-back atmosphere, yet offers the tourist or resident an ever-wider choice of places to dine-out, tapear (drink and tapa-bar crawl) and dance the night away Sadly the "cine de verano" (open-air summer cinema) is no longer a part of the evening entertainment but enthusiasts of this wonderful institution can go to Cine Las Palmeras in the neighboring village of La Cala. For the latest in air-conditioned, high-tech, a super-sound, ergonomic-seated cinema, the Rincón Centro Comercial (opened 2002) offers twenty screens.

Rincon de la Victoria's greatest asset is its lively urban sea front and beach. From the westernmost cliff top, marked by a Moorish watch-tower, the view sweeps down the length of the sandy beach, past the clutter of blue and white fishing boats, chiringuitos (fish restaurants on the beach), palm trees, the occasional cluster of thatched sunshades, and the endless to-ing and fro-ing of promenaders, cyclists and joggers.

The sea front itself, recently rebuilt and improved, stretches from one end of the town to the other. Two popular walks with Rinconites are along the sea front to La Cala, and to the shrine of the town's patron, the Virgin del Carmen, embedded in the rock at the westernmost tip of the beach.

Apart from sea, sun, sand and succulent seafood, Rincón does have one or two sights worth seeing. The Casa Fuerte (fort) set in one of the towns few green spaces doubles as an art gallery and occasional concert chamber. Dating back to the reign of Carlos III, the fortress was built in 1733 as part of the coastal defense against English pirate attacks. Most visitors to the town take a trip to the famous Treasure Cave, "la Cueva del Tesoro", located just outside the town in the residential area of El Cantal.

Like every other village and town in Andalucia, Rincón has its fair share of fiestas and festivals. The feria takes place in July and last for five days, coming to an end on the 16th, the day of the Virgen del Carmen. A folkloric spectacle of flower-decked thrones and boats, sailors and fishermen, cheering and veneration, rocket flares and fireworks, this is a festival not to be missed.

We stayed the night at the Hotel Gastiez which was very nice. It is interesting to note that all the hotels we stayed at were 4.5 & 5 star hotels. All the rooms were lovely and most had the most magnificent tiled bathrooms or Aseo as they are called. But all the rooms are smaller than American hotel rooms and most of them have inadequate air conditions. Also the minute you take your key out of the wall slot all the electric and the a/c stops. We figured that out quickly and kept one key in the slot and used the other to get in and out with.

Dinner was a traditional meal of vegetable stew and fish and the start of the continuous flow of flan that followed us wherever we went each night for dinner. It was noted that it is very expensive here. Victoria is in the Basque country. We had looked forward to our visit to the Basque country, but we did not get to see much of it since we drove through most of it.

Day 5 June 21, 2005 Vitoria-Bilbao-San Sebastian-Pamplona.
This morning we traveled to Bilbao, the great port city of the Basque region for a visit to the GUGGENHEIM MUSEUM, an amazing feat of construction created by the North American architect Frank O. Gehry. I think today is the Summer Solstice and it is cooler and very overcast. We enjoyed the Guggenheim and all its exhibits, especially, "The Puppy" which is a 4 story dog outside make completely of a frame that holds thousands of potted flowers. This was created by artist Jeff Koons in 1992 and was only supposed to be there for 2 years. However, it was so popular that they just keep replacing the flowers all year round.

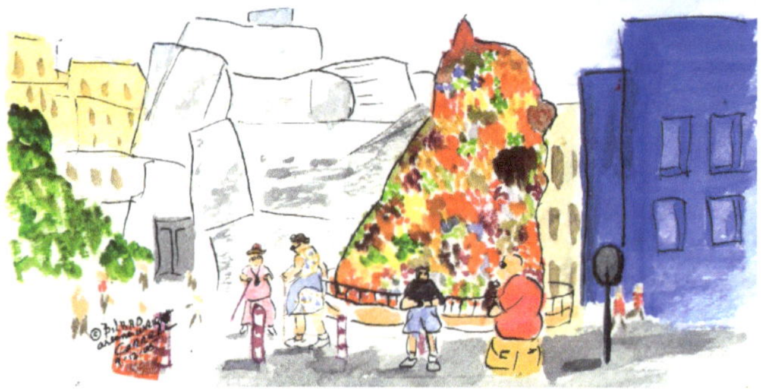

Back on the bus and we head for and stop in lovely San Sebastian, the "Pearl of the Cantabrian Coast" and Spain's gastronomical capital, before arriving in Pamplona, at the foot of the Pyrenees. We bought some wonderful bread and cheese in an underground market. Each day we have our wine on the bus. Not everyone, just us. We buy 2 or 3 bottles every other day and drag it with us. The wine is so inexpensive and good. We got some great red wine on sale for 79 cents a bottle and 2 bottles of Cava for only $2.19 each. Cava is Spain's answer to champagne.

San Sebastian is also known as the famous aristocratic beach resort of great reputation during last century still conserves its exclusive and cosmopolitan ambience. Its beautiful buildings and excellent beaches still today make it a privileged holiday destination. It is also herald as the most glamorous city in Spain. San Sebastian in the Basque Country of Northern Spain is a place where people live life to the fullest. Indulging in up to six meals a day, the people of San Sebastian really do know their food. The city has more bars and restaurants per head of population than anywhere else on earth.

Originally founded in the 12th century, San Sebastian is the culinary capital of Spain.

Today the heart of the city is Constitution Square, and one of the first things you'll notice upon visiting is the numbers on the balconies. This dates back to the middle Ages when the Square was used for bullfighting. These numbered rooms with a bird's eye view of the action were rented by curious spectators.

A short stroll away at the Farmers' Markets is the essence of San Sebastian quality cuisine - fresh local produce. The Spanish believe eating is an adventure to be shared and a way of bringing people together.

While in San Sebastian, I went into McPepido's (McDonald's) and used the men's room since the ladies line was incredible and besides there was no one in the men's room!

We arrived in Pamplona which is the capital of Navarra and the end of the Basque Country. Yes, *this* is the town of the "Running of Bulls", one of the most famous events in all the country. Great American writer *Ernest Hemingway* loved Pamplona for this spectacle which is part of the popular festival of *Sanfermines*, as he loved bullfighting in general, and this town is one of its centers. We were too early for the annual running of the bulls. However, I could just envision this painting of us there with George saying, "For God's sake, Barbara, get the hell out of the way!"

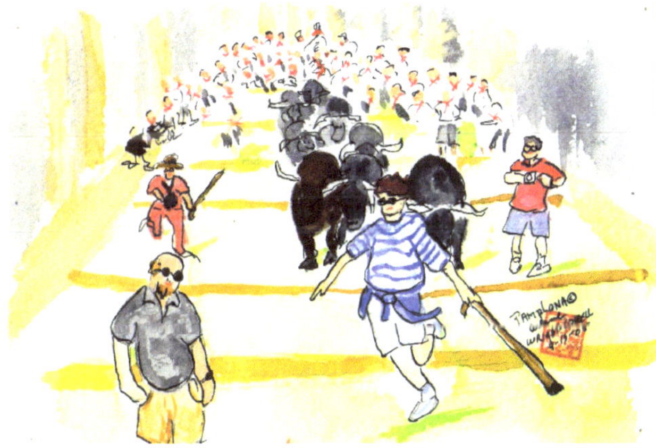

But also if you shouldn't like to participate in something as spectacular as mentioned above, this well cared-for northern-Spanish town certainly has something interesting to offer. It's very well conserved historical center for instance, or the picturesque mountain ranges of the region *Navarra*, with some of the most original folklore of all Spain. And to the *gourmets* it won't be anything new if I tell you that here are growing some really fine wines. The 4 of us can attest to that. Well, 3 of us can since Barbara doesn't drink any.

Pamplona is at the foot of the Pyrenees. Long day and we were glad to get into our hotel. Dinner consisted of duck which I had never eaten before and the most wonderful gazpacho soup that was like a pale pink puree.

Day 6 June 22nd 2005 Pamplona-Saragossa-Barcelona.
We are up and out and busing it by 8:00 am. These early mornings are so hard on Barbara. We enjoy vistas of Rioja wine country and the fertile Ebro Valley on the way to Saragossa. A local expert took us to Plaza del Pilar, one of Spain's grandest squares. Here we visited OUR LADY OF THE PILLAR and the even more spectacular LA SEO.

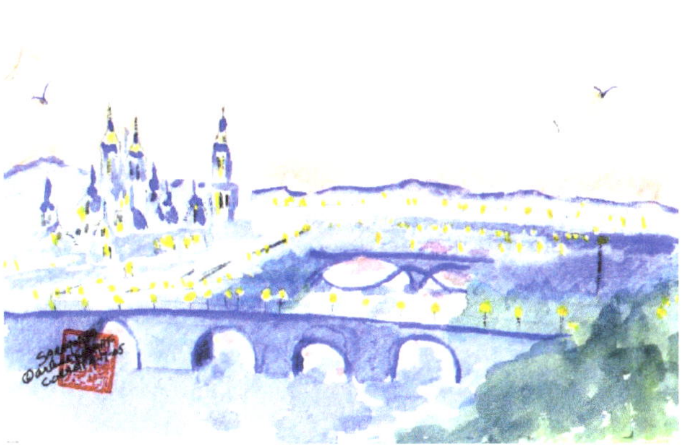

The most dominating features of the city include the stone bridge (**Puente de Piedra**), the original was of Roman construction, although re-built several times, it stands proudly over the River Ebro at its widest point. Today's bridge was last built in 1813 and features Italian, Basque and French architectural features.

The **Basilica of our lady of El Pilar** (El Pilar), stands at the foot of the bridge and is the most important structure in the whole of the region. This impressive structure was built in 1681 to commemorate the legendary appearance of the Virgin to the Apostle, James, on the site of a previous Visigothic church to Santa Maria.

Back on the bus through the rustic Catalonian landscape as we head towards Barcelona, Spain's second-largest city and the host of the Olympic Games of 1992. We had a great time the last time the 4 of us were in Barcelona so we were looking forward to it again. During the drive in we saw whole villages with many houses and a big center church in each one that could be purchased for 10,000 to 15,000 Euros. Most of the homes were handyman specials.

During one of our rest stops we had a mushroom and garlic potato frittata which was excellent. George served the wine! We are in the Cava region!

Day 7 June 23rd, 2005 Barcelona.
Today we go sightseeing with a local guide who tells us all about the Columbus Monument, elegant tree-lined Ramblas and Plaza de Cataluna, historic buildings along Paseo de Gracia, the Church of the Holy Family, a panoramic view of the city and harbor from Monjuich Hill, and a visit to the cathedral of SANTA EULALIA. Afternoon was at our leisure. An optional excursion to Montserrat was by-passed by the 4 of us and we just had a great time revisiting many of the places we had been to before including the Ramblas with all its activity and the great open air market that is off one of the side streets.

Here is the Mercat de la Boqueria; a large and colorful market on the Ramblas. This is our second visit to this market in two years and we are always dazzled by the brilliance of color from the fruits and vegetables in its stalls. This is where we get great olives, strawberries, and wonderful bread. Plus again great, inexpensive wine!

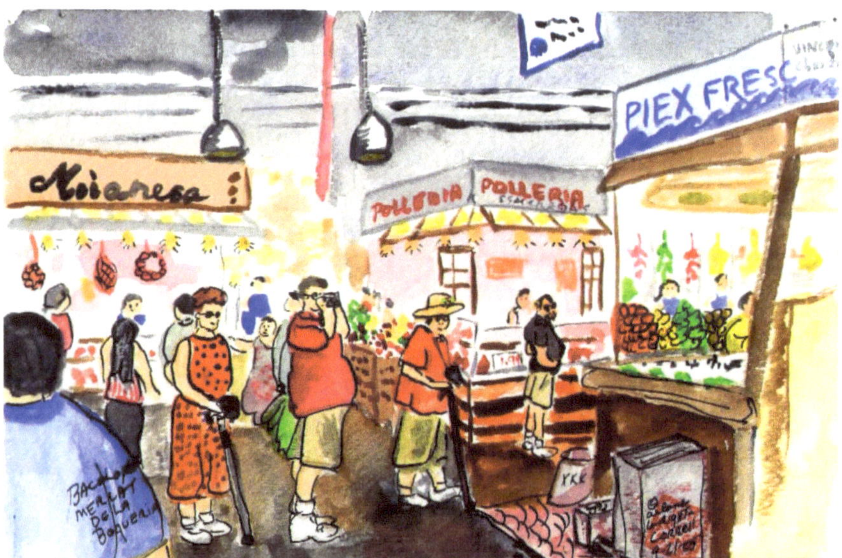

We passed on the city tour since we did that last time we were here and also on Gaudi stuff in a "been there, done that" attitude and the Monserrat Monastery tour during our 2 day stay here so we could just be travelers for awhile instead of tourists! We sit in sidewalk cafes on the Ramblas and watch the world go by. We stop in the late afternoon for tapas.

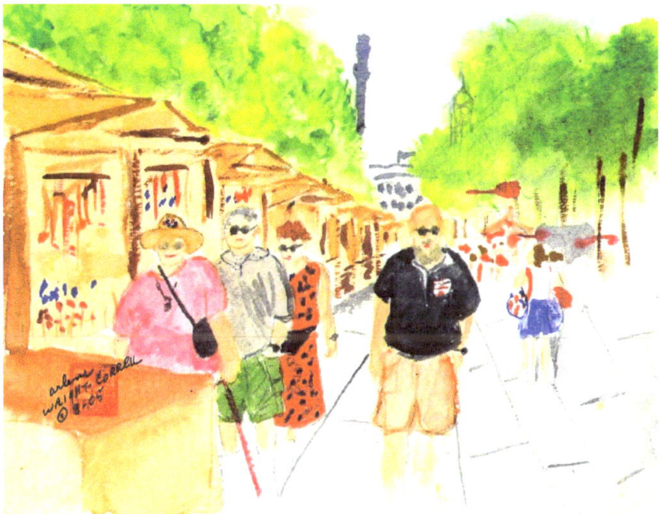

Arlene, Carl, Barbara, and George strolling along the Ramblas

We stayed at the Hotel Ambassador for 2 nights, which is 2 city blocks from where the bus can drop us off. What a walk with carry on stuff! The shower in our room is terrible and again the a/c leaves a lot to be desired. Again we are fed chicken and potatoes and the chef is not to be complimented.

The 2nd night we decide to find a restaurant and we tried Shrimp Paella which leaves a lot to be desired the way it is authentically made in Spain. With that in mind we canceled the Torremolinos dinner which is supposed to be famous for its paella. I figured out why so many people eat outdoors of the restaurants. When one eats inside, one is charged for table cloths, napkins etc, per person and that is above your meal plus the tip.

Day 8 June 24, 2005 Barcelona-Valencia.

The hotel redeems itself this morning with a Cava (champagne) breakfast. My kind of way to start the day and George agrees with me.

The morning drive along the coast past Tarragona and Castellon to Valencia, once a royal capital and now a sunny garden city surrounded by orange groves. The Tarragona and Castellon countryside is loaded with artichokes, rice fields which are planted in March and harvested in September. They grow Saffron rice and Valencia Oranges. We see many acres of very old olive trees and almond trees which were all hit by a rare frost this past winter. We discover when one sees square turrets on castles it indicates they were built by the Arabs. Christians built round turrets.

Valencia is where Spain's most famous food right where it was born: "Paella Valenciana"

Then Valencia is of course the city where "El Cid", Spain's national hero, fought against the Moors, and popular festivals in the city and many villages around still remind of this epoch.

Valencia's Roman, Moorish, and Spanish history come alive on our afternoon tour. We start out with a panoramic drive past landmarks such as the Town Hall, La Lonja, the Bull Ring, and the massive gateway towers of Serranos and Quart. We also visited LA SEO CATHEDRAL and the FALLAS MUSEUM.

We stayed at the Hotel Astoria Palace in Valencia. We took a walking tour and had Margarita Pizzas for lunch at a lovely sidewalk café. We went back to the hotel and Barbara went up for a nap, passing on the city tour which the 3 of us took. We saw the buildings of the Arts and Science, Basilica and Cathedrals, plus the museum of ceramics while George was off on his own exploring expedition.

Day 9 June 25, 2005 Valencia-Granada.
We depart Valencia heading toward Granada. We move further along the coastline to Alicante then inland towards the mountains where we see Troglodyte cave dwellings hollowed out of the soft tufa stone near Guadix and Purullena come into focus as you travel through one of Spain's most characteristic landscapes. Rugged Mora Pass finally leads us to the splendors of Granada.

Granada was first settled by native tribes in the prehistoric period, and was known as Ilbyr. When the Romans colonized southern Spain, they built their own city here and called it Illibris. The Arabs, invading the peninsula in the 8th century, gave it its current name of Granada. It was the last Muslim city to fall to the Christians in 1492, at the hands of Queen Isabel of Castile and her husband Ferdinand of Aragon.

One of the most brilliant jewels of universal architecture is the Alhambra, a series of palaces and gardens built under the Nazari Dynasty in the 14th C. This mighty compound of buildings – including the summer palace called Generalife, with its fountains and gardens - stands at the foot of Spain's highest mountain range, the Sierra Nevada, and overlooks the city below and the fertile plain of Granada.

At the centre of the Alhambra stands the massive Palace of Charles V, an outstanding example of Spanish Renaissance architecture. Other major Christian monuments found in the city are the Cathedral, including the Royal Chapel where Isabel and Ferdinand lie buried, the Monastery of La Cartuja and many churches built by Moorish craftsmen after the Reconquest, in Granada's unique "mudéjar" style. The hill facing the Alhambra is the old Moorish casbah or "medina", called the Albaicin, a fascinating labyrinth of narrow streets and whitewashed houses with secluded inner gardens, known as "cármenes". The Plaza de San Nicolas, at the highest point of the Albaicin, is famous for its magnificent view of the Moorish palace.

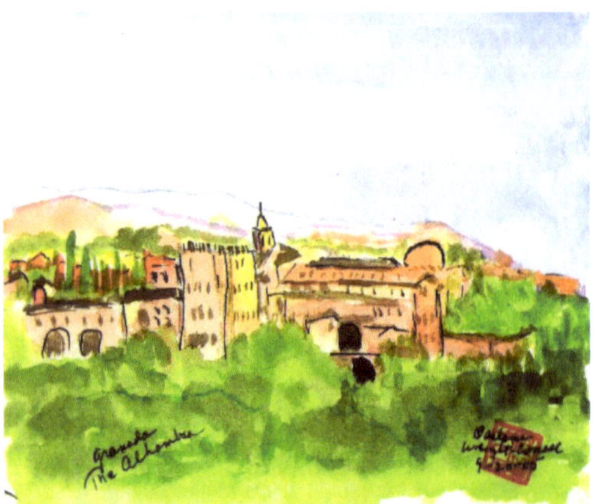

The name Alhambra comes from an Arabic root which means "red or crimson castle", perhaps due to the hue of the towers and walls that surround the entire hill of La Sabica which by starlight is silver but by sunlight is transformed into gold. But there is another more poetic version, evoked by the Moslem analysts who speak of the construction of the Alhambra fortress "by the light of torches", the reflections of which gave the walls their particular coloration. Created originally for military purposes, the Alhambra was an *alcazaba* (fortress), an *alcázar* (palace) and a small *medina* (city), all in one. This triple character helps to explain many distinctive features of the monument.

There is no reference to the Alhambra as being a residence of kings until the 13th century, even though the fortress had existed since the 9th century. The first kings of Granada, the Zirites, had their castles and palaces on the hill of the Albaicin, and nothing remains of them. The Nasrites were probably the emirs who built the Alhambra, starting in 1238.

The founder of the dynasty, Muhammed Al-Ahmar, began with the restoration of the old fortress. His work was completed by his son Muhammed II, whose immediate successors continued with the repairs. The construction of the palaces (called *Casa Real Vieja*, "old Royal House or Palace") dates back to the 14th century and is the work of two great kings: Yusuf I and Muhammed V. To the first we owe, among others, the *Cuarto de Comares* (Chamber of Comares), the *Puerta de la Justicia* (Gate of Justice), the Baths and some towers. His son, Muhammed V, completed the beautification of the palaces with the *Cuarto de los Leones* (Chamber of the Lions), as well as other rooms and fortifications.

The Alhambra became a Christian court in 1492 when the Catholic Monarchs (Ferdinand and Isabel) conquered the city of Granada. Later, various structures were built for prominent civilians' also military garrisons, a church and a Franciscan monastery. Emperor Charles V, who spent several months in Granada, began the construction of the palace which bears his name and made some alterations to the interior buildings. These measures were to cause interminable controversy often motivated by political agendas. The remaining Austrian kings did not forget the monument and have left their own more discreet impressions on it.

During the 18th century and part of the 19th, the Alhambra fell into neglect and was to see its salons converted into dung heaps and taverns, occupied by thieves and beggars. "Thus bats defile abandoned castles, and the reality of Spanish criminals and beggars destroy the illusion of this fairy palace of the Moors;" writes Richard Ford. As the crowning blow, Napoleon's troops, masters of Granada from 1808 until 1812, were to convert the palaces into barracks during one retreat they mined the towers and blew up part of them. Two of them, the *Torre de Siete Suelos* and the *Torre de Agua* were left in ruins. And so the incredible neglect continued, until 1870 when the Alhambra was declared a national monument. Travelers and romantic artists of all countries had railed against those who scorned the most beautiful of their monuments. Since that date and up to now, the Alhambra, protected, restored, cared for and even improved, has been preserved for the pleasure and admiration of all.

Alcazaba

This is the oldest part of the Alhambra, reconstructed upon the ruins of a castle in the 9th century. The most solid towers are those of the Homenaje situated to the south, and the Quebrada at the northeast angle. The most elaborate interior is the Torre de las Armas.

However all are surpassed by the impressive Torre de la Vela. Its bell is rung on special festive occasions by young girls in the hope of warding off spinsterhood - dated though this sounds these days! This is the tallest tower of the walled enclosure, and the panorama seen from here extends towards unlimited horizons. Its silhouette is a significant symbol to the people of Granada.

At the entrance of the Alcazaba is the delightful Jardín de los Adarves, also called Jardin de los Poetas. From its battlements our gaze is drawn to the towers of the hill in the foreground. They are the Torres Bermejas (red or crimson towers), the "castle of great worth" of a famous border ballad. Their bewitching name is evoked in the music of Albéniz or Joaquín Rodrigo.

La Casa Real (The royal house or palace)
This is comprised of several palace groups with a series of courts and structures surrounding them which were born out of transitory or ornamental necessity. Since the 16th century these Nasrite alcázares (palaces) have been designated the Casa Real Vieja (Old Royal House) in order to distinguish them from the Christian buildings.

The Alhambra contains the three divisions usually found in a Moslem palace, including a reception salon and the royal apartments Chamber of the Lions. This spectacular chamber is the work of Muhammed V and illustrates the most beautiful possibilities of Granada Moslem art. Throughout this chamber a subtle air of femininity and daintiness is sensed, in keeping with the function of these private apartments, devoted to the placid enjoyment of home and family life.

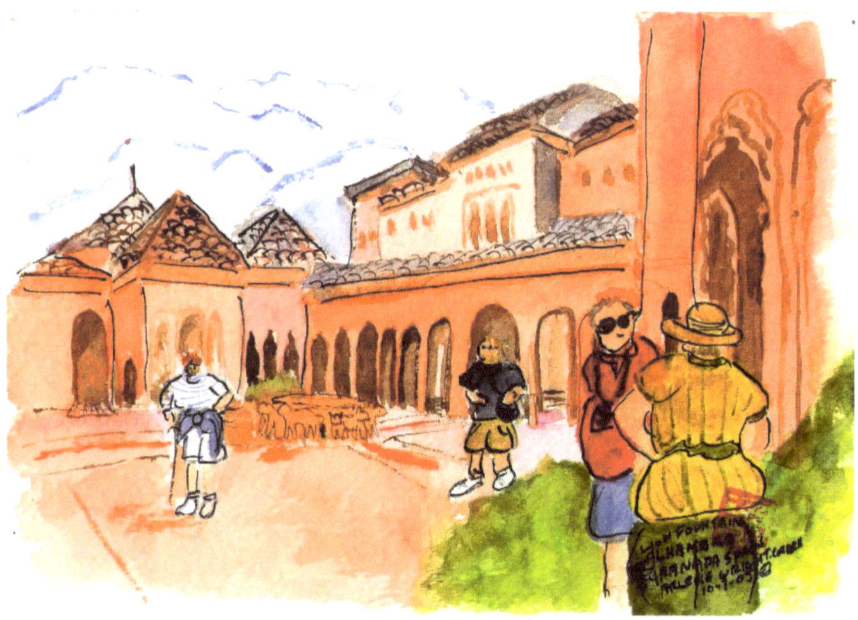

The Court of the Lions is characterized by its profound originality, a harmonious merging of East and West. It has been compared to a grove of 124 palm trees, most with double columns, around the oasis of the central fountain with its twelve lions. The twelve-sided marble fountain rests upon the backs of the lions. Water, as essential as well as a decorative element acquires here an exceptional importance. It ascends and spills from the basin, which has been compared with the 'sea of bronze' of Solomon's Temple, to the mouths of the lions, from which it is distributed throughout the courtyard. A lovely qasida (ode) by Ibn Zamrak circles the rim of the basin.

Four large halls border the courtyard. The first, entering from the Court of the Myrtles, is the Sala de los Mozárabes, whose name is perhaps derived from the three stalactite arches which form the entrance to the Court of the Lions. To the south is the Sala de Abencerrajes, famous in legend with a gateway decorated with lazo (ornamental knots). Light penetrates the hall through 16 graceful fretwork windows. On the east side is the Sala de los Reyes which is unusual and resembles a theatrical set, divided in three sections which correspond to three lovely porticos, separated by double arches of mozárabes (stalactites).

North of the Court of the Lions is the Sala de las Dos Hermanas, so called because of the two large marble flagstones flanking the central fountain and spout. The adjoining hall is the Sala de los Ajimeces with two balconies overlooking the Garden of Daraxa. Between these two balconies is the Mirador de Daraxa, dressing room and bedroom of the Sultana and a delightful retreat in this secluded section of the palace, in the style of a bay window or mirador.

The last hall gives access to the Peinador de la Reina, also called the Tocador. An open gallery and an airy little tower, it was once designed as the residence of the Empress Isabel and later of Isabel of Parma. Some restored frescoes portray scenes of Charles V's expedition to La Goleta. In the Christian Alhambra within the Alhambra enclosure there are also monuments which are exclusively Western. For example, in the Jardines de los Mártires there was once a monastery of the barefoot Carmelite order.

The Church of St Mary is built upon the site where the royal mosque formerly stood. The Monastery of St Francis, which is now a parador, was erected upon an Arab palace and has the additional merit and sentimental value of having housed the temporary sepulcher of the Catholic Monarchs - Ferdinand and Isabella, until their transfer to the Capilla Real. Palace of Charles V The Palacio de Carlos V or Casa Real Nueva as it is better known, was commissioned by the Emperor in an endeavor to emulate the Palace of the defeated Moslems and also to provide for himself a habitable residence. Construction was started in 1527 under the direction of Pedro Machuca, who had studied with Michelangelo in Italy. The palace is built in the form of a square and comprised of two main parts: the first, in Tuscan style, and the second with Ionic pillars.

The Sacromonte hill, which overlooks the city from the North, is famous for its cave dwellings, once the home of Granada's large gypsy community.
The name Granada is ancient and mysterious. It may mean "great castle", for the Roman fortress which once stood on the Albaicin Hill. When the Moors came here, the town was largely inhabited by Jews, for which they called it Garnat-al-Yahud - Granada of the Jews. The Jews are said to have been one of the first peoples to settle in Spain, even before the Romans.
To me, this was truly worth the whole trip.

Generalife of Granada
The word 'Generalife' has been translated as 'garden of paradise', 'orchard' or 'garden of feasts'.

After the city was conquered, the Generalife was granted by the Catholic Monarchs to the Granada Venegas family. The promenade leads to the Patio de la Acequia which is the most celebrated spot and the heart and soul of the palace grounds. On the western side there is a gallery of 18 arches. The northern portico is called the Mirador and has five arches in front, slender and stylized and three behind made of marble with stalactite capitals. Through the north portico is the Patio de los Cipreses, with a pool in the centre. The distribution of the small ponds is charming with their frames of oleander and myrtle.

A stone step leads to the Upper Gardens which were once olive groves and today boast a handsome esplanade and modern gardens. Here is the unusual stairway with its cascading waterfalls which was described by Navagiero as early as the 16th century. The stairway leads to a modern, uninteresting edifice of several stories. At the far end is the large open air stage where the annual International Festival of Music and Dance is performed.

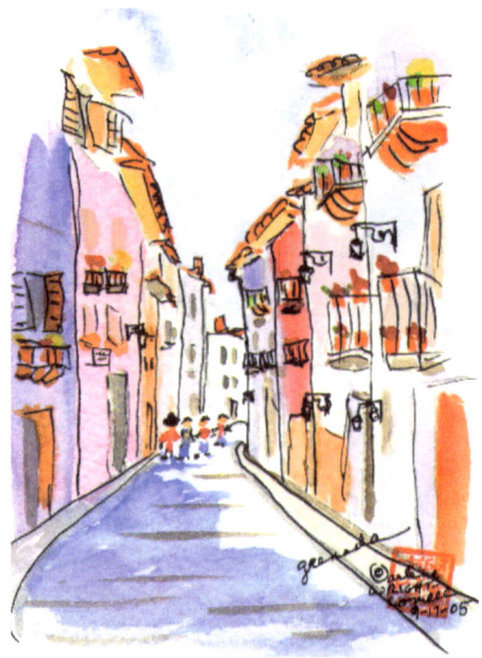

This was a hard day of walking for me and especially for Barbara. George had to take her back to the bus in a taxi.

Day 10 June 26, 2005 Granada-Torremolinos.
In the afternoon it was a short drive down to the Costa del Sol and our hotel in Torremolinos. We had balcony side by side rooms that overlooked the Mediterranean Sea and we all got a chance to sit outside and sip wine and enjoy the view. When we first arrived there the beaches were packed but by 7 pm there was no one on them. The Costa de Sol is a very popular resort area.

We walked the beach area and got some nice ceramic tiles that say "Casa Correll" over our kitchen windows and one that says, "Arlene" for my art studio. I love tiles from different places. We ate in a lovely sidewalk café right on the beach.

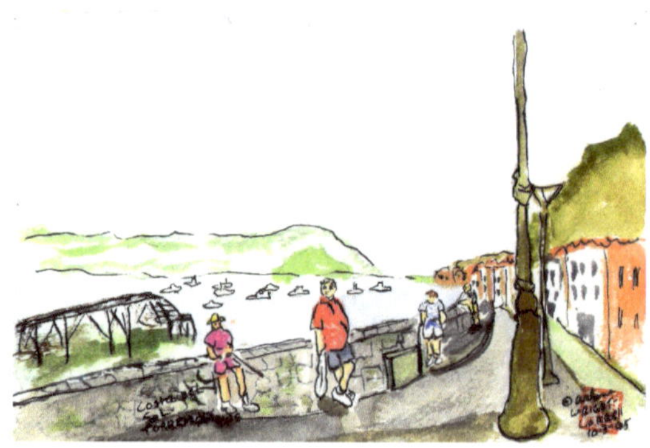

Day 11 June 27, 2005 Torremolinos-Gibraltar-Seville.

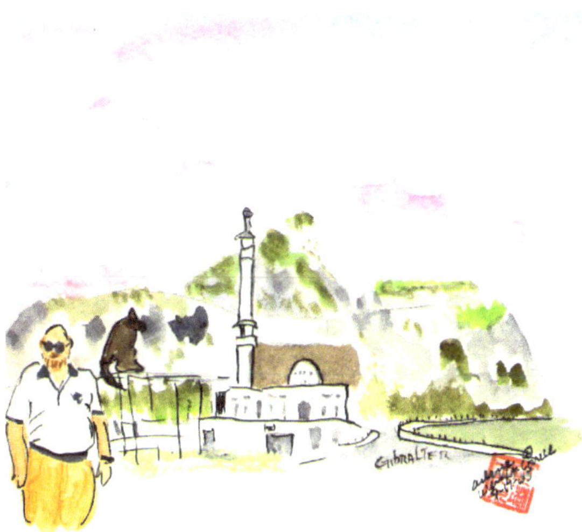

We motored along the Costa del Sol to the rock fortress of Gibraltar, in British hands since 1704. There is a lot of turbulent history, but by the time we arrived I had become under the weather and stayed in a small café where I was able to drink chamomile tea while George, Barbara and Carl went to see the Moorish Castle, and ST. MICHAEL'S CAVES and of course, the colony of Barbary apes. While over in Gibraltar they were detained coming back with a bomb scare.

Gibraltar is rich in history; to the early Greek and Roman's Gibraltar was one of the two Pillars erected by Hercules to mark the edge of the world. For many citizens of the USA, the "Rock" has been permanently marked into their childhood through repeated viewing of an insurance company advertisement that touted the company to be" as stable as the Rock of Gibraltar!"

Many people don't feel a visit to Gibraltar is worth the time as it's not Spain and it's not really like visiting the British Isles. Still, Carl and the others found their visit to the Rock of Gibraltar to be a welcome relief from touring another Cathedral or Castle.
One has to go through custom when leaving Spain to enter Gibraltar since it is a British possession. Once you got through customs you get to walk across the airport runway. If you don't see any cars crossing with you, do look for the crosswalk light and verify the way is clear with no planes landing.

Carl and George like to walk, but for Barbara to really experience a place she said she had to huff and puff a little, and Gibraltar provides a lot of opportunity for huffing and puffing. If you're a walker, ignore all the tour by car offers and walk up the main street, through the shopping district, until you get to the cable car. The Cable Car drops you off at the top of the rock and you can use it to return to the bottom or just walk down as we did. Plan on walking for about 6 or more hours to see the Rock (even though you start at the top, this is up, as well as some down walking).

Finally the group returned and we then on through the sunny sherry wine region on the Costa de la Luz to vibrant, festive Seville.

Day 12 June 28, 2005 Seville.
We had a local expert's account of the Andalusian city's role in Roman times, its conquest by the Moors in 712, and its contribution to the discovery of the New World. We saw MARIA LUISA PARK and the Plaza de España, the Gold Tower on the Guadalquivir River, and the fine baroque building that is now the university but used to

be the tobacco factory of Carmen fame. We visited the CATHEDRAL with Columbus' tomb, the world's largest Gothic edifice. Finally stroll through the narrow lanes of the charming Santa Cruz Quarter. The rest of the day was at leisure. We had an authentic Andalusian night out when we went to see flamenco show. We were enthralled with this show. It was amazing. So when I painted this picture I decided to add the 4 amigos dancing along with them. Barbara and I with our walking sticks, Carl with the two dancing ladies and George just kicking up his heels.

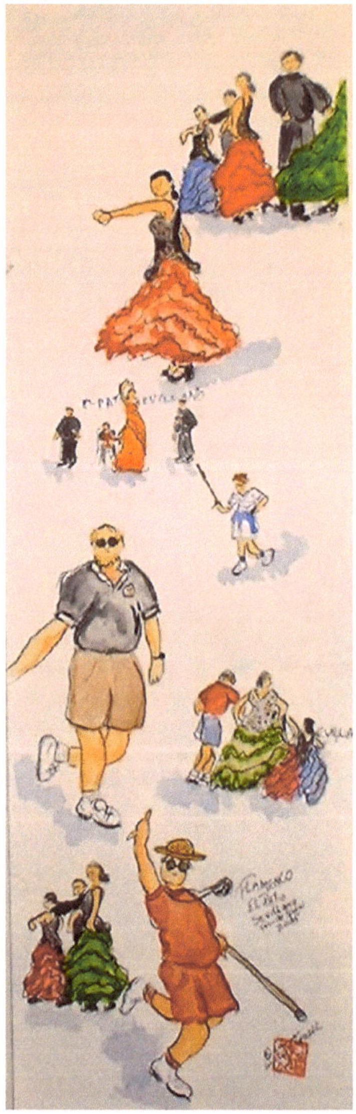

According to legend, Sevilla was founded by Hercules and its origins are linked with the Tartessian civilization. It was called Hispalis under the Romans and Isbiliya with the Moors. Its high point in its history was following the discovery of America.

Sevilla lies on the banks of the Guadalquivir and is one of the largest historical centers in Europe, it has the minaret of **La Giralda**, the cathedral (one of the largest in Christendom), and the Alcázar Palace. Part of its treasure include Casa de Pilatos, the Town Hall, Archive of the Indies (where the historical records of the American continent are kept), the Fine Arts Museum (the second largest picture gallery in Spain) , plus convents, parish churches and palaces.

It has hosted two international exhibitions (1929 and 1992) and is the administrative capital of Andalucía. The quarter of Triana on the other side of the river, La Macarena, Santa Cruz and San Bartolomé, the street of Las Sierpes, plus La Maestranza bullring, **María Luisa Park** and the riverside walks are all representative images of Sevilla

Here we are at the Spanish Square or the Plaza de España.
Laid out in 1929 for an abortive 'Fair of the Americas', the Plaza de España and adjoining Maria Luisa Park are among the most pleasant - and impressive - public spaces in Spain. They are an ideal place to spend the middle part of the day, just ten minutes' walk to the east of the cathedral.

Today, the plaza mainly comprises government offices while the surrounding moat can be best appreciated by renting out a rowing boat. A vast semicircular complex with fountains, monumental staircases and a mass of tile work, it is quite spectacular. There is a tiled alcove named after each of the provinces of Spain. Visitors like to have their photo taken in their home province.

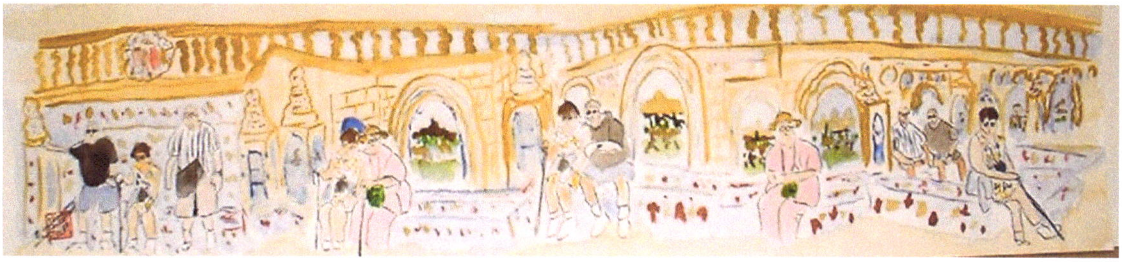

Carl, Barbara & George – Barbara & me ---------- Barbara & Carl ----me --------- George, Carl & Barbara.

Seville has a rich and fascinating history. The Romans governed the whole of Spain for more than six centuries. Their first colony was Italica which may still be visited today. The Romans changed the face of the countryside and towns, building aqueducts and long straight roads to link the major towns. Today some of the best preserved artifacts from this period can be found at the city's magnificent Archaeological Museum.

But it was the Moslem civilization which was to have the most lasting impact on the city. Their reign lasted for nearly 800 years in Andalucia from 711 until 1492 when the Catholic monarchs defeated the Moslem kingdom of Granada.

Some of the city's most magnificent buildings stand as a legacy to this era, including the Torre del Oro, Torre de Plata, Giralda, Patio de los Naranjos, the area of Triana, the Macarena Walls and the Alcazar. Later the Mudejares used their skill to create beautiful Moorish-style buildings, such as the Palacio Pedro 1, part of Seville's Reales Alcazres. There are several Mudejar churches dating from this period, including the Iglesia de San Marcos, the Iglesia de Santa Catalina and the Church of San Pedro.

Interestingly, Mudejar architecture continued long after the Moslem period, one of the best examples being the Casa de Pilatos, one of the most beautiful buildings you can visit in Seville. The city walls and gates offer an insight into the history over the ages.
After the fall of Granada to the Christians, Spain entered an era of expansion and prosperity. The conquest of the New World made Seville one of the most affluent cities in Europe, but much of this wealth was squandered on wars by the Hapsburg kings. The 13 year War of the Spanish Succession saw Bourbons on the throne in place of the Hapsburgs and, under the Treaty of Utrecht, the loss of Gibraltar to the British. Later ties with France dragged Spain into the Napoleonic Wars.

Following the Battle of Trafalgar, the Spanish King, Carlos 1V abdicated and Napoleon Bonaparte placed his brother, Joseph on the Spanish throne. The Peninsula War ensued and, with British help, the French were driven out of Spain. After the Bourbon restoration, Spain weakened by further strife, began to lose her colonies.

By the 18th century, Spain had fallen into economic decline and in the 19th and early 20th centuries poverty led to political conflict and ultimately to civil war.
Many of the more recent historic buildings date from the 1929 Ibero-American Exposition of 1929, including the Plaza de España and the Parque Maria Luisa.

In 1992 this event was repeated when Expo took place again in Seville, attracting thousands of visitors from around the world.

Day 13 June 29, 2005 Seville-Toledo-Madrid.

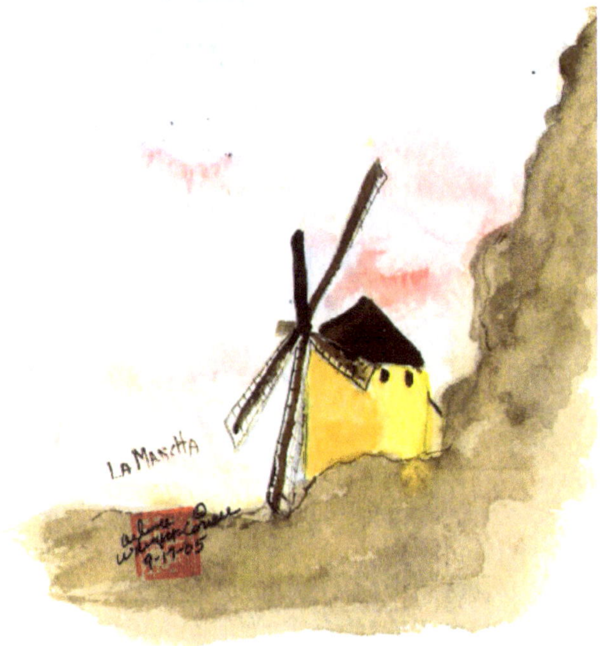

The lush valley of the Guadalquivir River gives way to the arid landscapes of Don Quixote's La Mancha. We stopped in the quaint little town of La Mancha. This region, also quite large in size, is located south of Madrid and occupies what was the southern part of the ancient kingdom of Castille, including the area known as La Mancha, universally famous as the setting for Miguel de Cervantes great novel "Don Quijote de la Mancha". There are 5 provinces in La Mancha. Toledo, Cuenca, Ciudad Real, Albacete, and Guadalajara

Today's highlight is Toledo. Spectacularly situated on a granite hill surrounded by a loop of the Tagus River, the ancient Castillian capital attracts more sightseers from all over the world than any other Spanish town. **Toledo**, the capital of this Autonomous Community, is without a doubt one of the densest monumental cities in the world.

Nearly all the different stages of Spanish art are represented in Toledo, which has Moorish-Mudejar-Jewish buildings, such as the Transito and Santa Maria la Blanca Synagogues; Gothic structures, such as the splendid cathedral: and Renaissance buildings. In the 16th century, the city became home to El Greco, and Toledo has many of his paintings, among which is "The Burial of the Count of Orgaz", his masterpiece which is housed in the Mudejar Church of Santo Tome. Among its many museums, of special note is the one located in the old Santa Cruz Hospital.

A resident expert was ready to take us to the Moorish bridge, an early SYNAGOGUE, the 13th-century GOTHIC CATHEDRAL, and the church of SANTO TOMÉ with one of El Greco's most famous paintings. This is a beautiful place. However, Barbara and I were getting worn out and told the fellows to go on by themselves and we would find a sidewalk café outside the walls. Carl elected to stay with us. George visited one of the Damascene steel workshops. We feel bad that we missed all the small winding streets this city is noted for. A real labyrinth where one can become easily lost. But we enjoyed our little rest and did our own walking outside the walls.

Day 14 June 20, 2005.
We are up at 3 am, our luggage out by 4 am and on our way to the airport for a early flight retracing our steps back to the good old US of A!

Since we had free round trip tickets from Louisville to NY, we could only return on July 3 or July 10th. George and Barbara were on their way to the PA place for the 4th and invited us. By now we were beat. We could get back on the 3rd in time for Jeff's birthday and the 4th here in KY if we flew out of Newark, NJ. However, that meant 3 nights in a hotel.

For the first time I went to Priceline.com and put in what I wanted to pay and how long we needed to stay. The price was right on a hotel we found with a shuttle to the airport and because we were staying more than one night we got a great price break and an upgrade.

George drove us to our final destination which was the Springhill Suites and we were delighted. We were given a $300.00 per night full suite for only $45.00 per night. Great service, great space, great incredible breakfasts that kept us full until dinner. They had a little market place kiosk in the lobby with tons of microwavable food to cover us for supper. We had 3 bottles of good Spanish wine we had brought back, so we never left the hotel. This hotel was considered a 2.5 star hotel in the USA and it had the Spain 4.5 & 5 star hotels beat by a country mile.

We arrived back in Munfordville about 2 p.m. of the 3rd and we sure were glad to be home. We had a great trip, but everyone is saying never again, at least not with that kind of escorted tour bus trip. George says we go back to renting cars, I say George is the designated driver; Carl says he is never leaving the United State again, and Barbara says maybe Montana next year!

This became a fun project all around. Not only did I get a lot out of the trip, I developed a new style of painting when I realized how I was going to do the sketches which were gouache water colors with Pen and Ink high lights. My notes taken during the bus ride lulls were decipherable upon returning home. (Travel light, don't drag a laptop with you, or paints, etc unless you are in your own car.) The project, upon returning home took me about 2 months to complete.

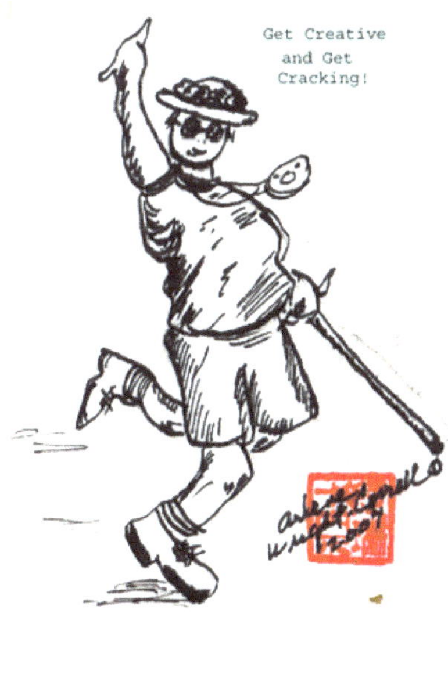

Not only do I have the paintings, the post cards, note cards, Giclee prints and tiles for sale, I have a good record of the trip and I have a chapter for this book. Not bad for someone who can't draw a straight line!

Chapter 8

How to create Pen & Ink Art & Calligraphy

After my stroke in September 1999 I decided I really needed something to bring myself back. My left side was the inflicted side and I was coming around. My left hand eventually became the only thing that was giving me a problem such as pins and needles, also my left big toe and when I got tired I slurred a lot. Fortunately for me I am right handed. I realized that part of my brain was damaged and I also realized that I needed to be doing things to stimulate the right and left sides of my brain again.

I remembered the simplicity of pen and ink sketches I had done in high school art and I also remember calligraphy which I had not done a lot of. However, I did remember that this was not an expensive creative avenue to get into, but it did require concentration and concentration in my mind stimulates the muscle between my ears called the brain.

So let's talk about Pen & Ink first.

The equipment needed for this art is so simple that one can carry it with them anywhere in a pocket, purse or backpack thus allowing you to sketch whenever the mood strikes you.

Here's a basic supply list for pens:

Dip Pens
Markers (which now come in a variety of colors)
Technical Pens
Ball Point Pens
Calligraphy Pens

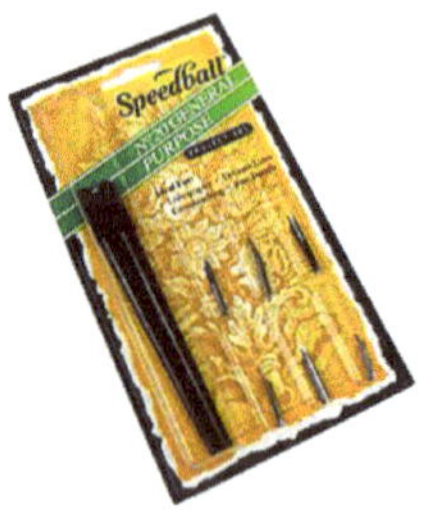

Dip Pens such as the crow quill dip pen is an adaptation of the earlier feather quill dip pens. It is simply a wooden or plastic holder with a removable steel nib.

This tool cleans very easily and is very inexpensive. You may use it for applying colored inks as well as black ink. The downside of crow quill dip pens is that they are limited in stroke direction, with a tendency to spatter or drip plus the re-dipping process interrupts the stroking rhythm.

Markers (which now come in a variety of colors)

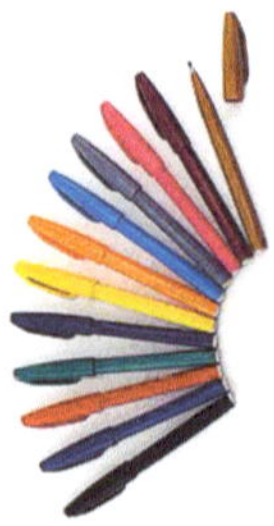

I find that felt-tip pens are great for doing little quick sketches simply because you don't have to wait for the ink to flow down to the nib and today's good markers can keep pace with even the fastest hand. They are made in a variety of colors, nib shapes and sizes and have a good degree of permanence. The down side of these is they are not capable of producing extremely fine lines when you require them and they are not to be considered replacements for the precise steel-nib pens.

Technical Pens

I consider the technical pen the best inking instrument available. It has a hollow metal nib, a self-contained ink supply either in the form of a pre-filled or refillable cartridge. Inside the hollow nib is a delicate wire and weight which shifts back and forth during use and that causes the ink to move forward. You should never remove the wire from the nib. The nibs are made of steel and are very durable on paper surfaces.

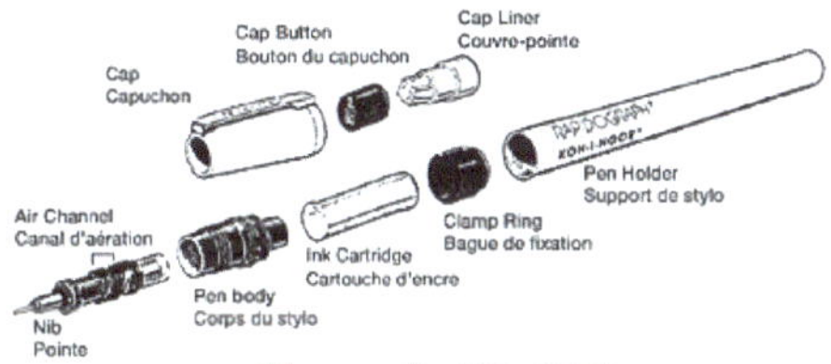

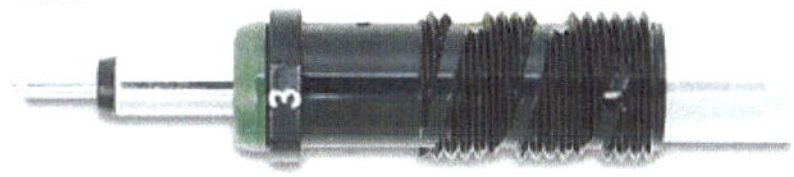

Ball Point Pens

Ball point pens come in all different colors, makes and models. I use them rarely, but they are handy to keep in the studio for the few times I do want to use them.

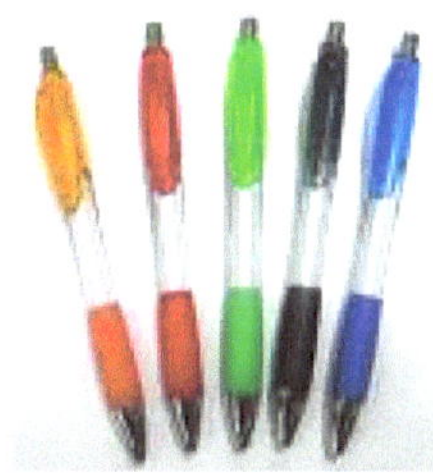

Here is my basic supply list for inks:
India Inks
Colored Inks

India Inks

Today, modern India inks are composed of water, finely ground carbon particles for rich black color with shellac or latex used as a binder. India inks have a shelf life of 2 to 5 years and the maker's different blends determine the ink's opacity, open pen time, surface drying time, adhesion and permanence. Old inks separate and are really not good to use or to try to reconstitute. When you discard them do it in an environmentally safe manner.

Years ago ink is available in two forms: stick and liquid. The stick ink is made from pine or oil carbon and glue. The mixture is poured into a mold and allowed to harden. Most sticks have some type of design on them. Sometimes it is a raised design, at other times the design is painted with colors. In the past, gold leaf or precious stones were often embedded, making the ink stick to precious to use and expensive. Today's liquid inks are really cheap ranging in price from $3.95 to $6.95 and these are the ones I prefer.

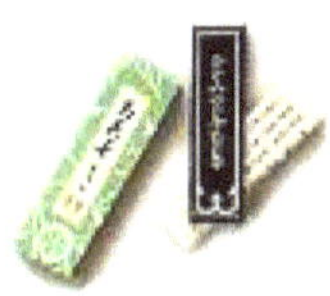

Ink sticks can still be purchased and they usually come from China varying in color tone and quality. Tones range from brownish to bluish, depending on the type of carbon used to make the ink. The decision to use a brown or blue tone is subjective one, based on which you like best.

Quality ranges from poor to excellent. Poor quality ink often has a grainy consistency and needs a lot of grinding before it turns black. Good quality-ink grinds easily, without scraping or scratching, and makes a rich, deep black.

I have never used any of these as my personal option is readymade bottle of ink. Again, there are a number of manufacturers and various qualities. Some of the manufacturers are unwilling to disclose their secret ingredients and formulae.

It is said one should stay away from India inks because they often contain shellac, which will degrade the hair of your brush. Use inks made in China, Japan, or Korea. However most of my India ink work is done with pens and I prefer the good old standards such as Speedball and Encre de Chine.

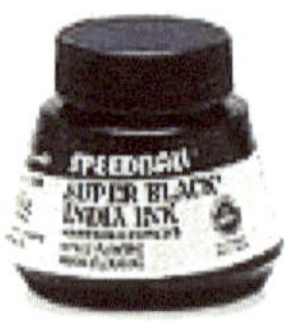

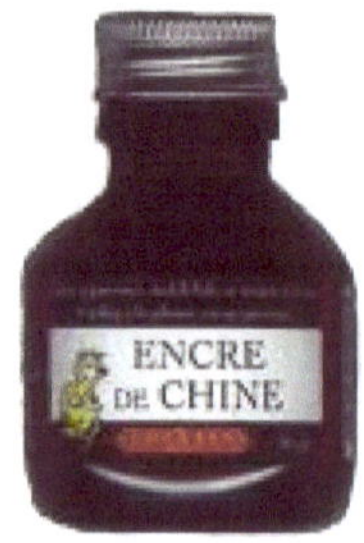

Colored Inks

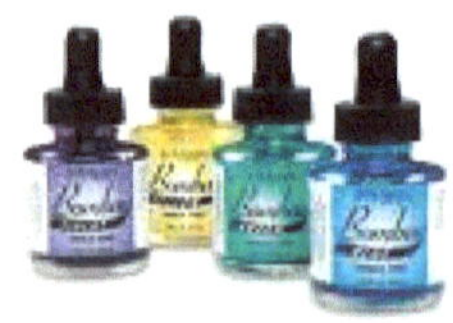

These are dye-based colored inks and might have a tendency to fade over time. Most colored inks are used in Technical pens.

I happen to like Dr. PH Martin's Black Star Matte & Hicarb Bombay India Inks, Bleed Proof White, Pen-White, Hydrus Fine Art Watercolor, Spectralite Private Collection Liquid Acrylic (for Fine Art), Iridescent Calligraphy Color for Rubber Stamping on Vinyl, vellum, acetate, all papers (including glossy stock) and board and all of these can be purchased on the net or in art stores. Again I prefer Hobby Lobby because I usually have a weekly 40% off coupon and many times this type of item might not be on sale when I need it.

Here is my basic supply list of surfaces I use for inking.

Art Boards
Bristol Boards
Mylar
Papers
Watercolor Paper
Textured Surfaces.

Pen and ink requires an absorbent paper with a firm polished texture which provides the best surface for pen and ink. Your pen should be able to glide over the paper without any want your resulting line to be precise in appearance and sharp-edged.

Calligraphy

Calligraphy is an easy and fun way to express yourself, especially your artistic style in handwriting. I don't do much of this any more. However, should it be something you want to experiment in then you can use some of the same tools as we used in Pen and Ink.

The supply list for Calligraphy is slightly longer and you will have to practice and practice. However, it will come quickly once you have the rules down as it takes basically no artistic talent.

Protractor
Ruler
Metal Straight Edge
Scissors
Compass
Dividers
Knife
Bone Folder
Pencils
Cow Gum
Eraser
PVA Glue
Masking Fluid
Cutting Mat
Brushes
Gum Arabic
Ruling Pen
Masking Tape

To make Basic Strokes just hold the pen at an angle of 30 degrees to the paper making sure you keep this angle consistent while writing and be sure your upright strokes don't slope.

One must concentrate on spacing the strokes evenly. Remember to look at the spaces between the strokes as well as the strokes themselves as this is an important trade secret to calligraphy.

Your curves should be balanced and appear to be upright. When you create straight strokes that lead into arches and curves, the straight strokes should be parallel and upright.

Your straight strokes should form a series of parallel lines with even spaces between them. Make sure your thick diagonal strokes and thin strokes are parallel to create triangles of while space that are equal and symmetrical.

It is important during use to clean the nib regularly on a cloth or tissue to prevent ink buildup.

Always clean your nibs and reservoirs after each use. I dip my immediately in a jar of water I keep handy at the work table. Cleaning each tool with an old toothbrush helps to keep them from rusting.

Go back to page 10 and see two of my pen and ink works. "The Medicine Man©" was done with Dr. PH Martin Inks and the "Hard to Kill©" was just a series of strokes with black India ink.

It is important to remember that is o.k. to fail or miss at some of these things. It is also important to remember to give yourself one or two hours a day to paint, draw, pen and ink or whatever creative thing you think you want to do.

It is never too late to start learning new things in the art world. Why go though life thinking your want to do something, but cannot. Foolish, we can learn anything we want to as long as we have the desire to do it.

I realize our lives are busy and seem to get busier as the years go on. You may be at a stage of your life where you are retiring and some of these arts may be something you wish to try. So go for it.

You just may need a change. Take charge of your life, your time and do not let your friends and family pooh pooh your new hobby or searches.

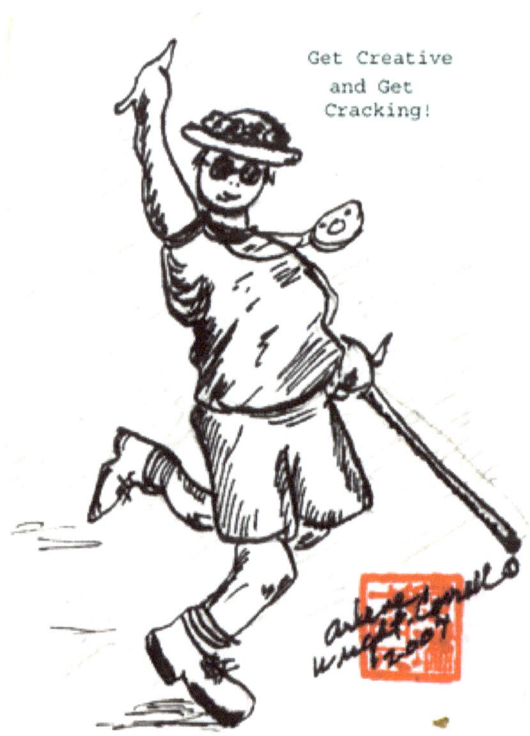

Chapter 9

How to Use Finishing Sprays and Vanishes

Now that you have finished several works of art you need to know how to protect your finished product and you need to feel secure about the quality of your work.

Today there are so many finishes to choose from varying from sprays and protective varnishes and these are great and convenient ways to keep your art from smearing or dirt and even sunlight.

Finishing sprays and varnishes come in matte, glossy or satin finishes and some are removable or allow you to rework your piece after application.

To reduce light reflections on ceramics, photographs and stencils use a matte finish. Dulling sprays reduces unwanted glare on reflective or shiny objects and make them much easier to photograph.

I want to digress for a minute and encourage you to make a book of your work right after it is done. I use postcard stock to make a hard copy photo. I also put them on a CD disc. I often send copies of these postcards to my friends and grand children as Artist's Trading Cards.

However let's get back to finishing sprays. Some sprays are designed to ease the process of working by improving the flow of paint and speeding up drying time. Just remember to read the labels to find out what spray does what.

I sometimes use a finishing spray during chalk, charcoal and pastel works when I want to set up a layer and may even do it several times to set up several layers. However, I always use a spray to seal all these types of works to prevent smudging and fading. I know this will keep my works well for years and years.

I use varnishes on oil paintings. I use a retouch vanish after finishing an oil painting and then about a year later, (providing I have not sold it) I apply Damar Varnish to seal it. You can use that or any other kind that you prefer. Just make sure it is a quality varnish because you want your end product to continue to look freshly painted conserving your colors and protect your painting from aging. You can also use these varnishes for finishing stained furniture, craft projects and frames.

When I do my scratch art or Claybord art, I always finish it off with a matte finish of Claybord Fixative. This is a very fast drying (in about 30 seconds) spray that allows you to display your Claybord art without glass. You can also use it on watercolors without glass. I like it because it will immediately dissolve any fingerprints I may have left on my Claybord work.

Gesso is a painting medium that comes ready mixed as a painting ground and you can apply 3 coats, each one in a different direction, on any surface to create a painting surface. Let it dry completely between coats and then lightly sand it before applying the next coat. Now you are ready to apply any kind of paint to your surface.

You can use many mediums on Acrylics.

Gloss medium can be used as a glazing medium or a painting medium or even as a finished coating to create a glossy appearance.

Matte medium can used glazing medium or a painting medium or even as a finished coating to create a Matte appearance.

Gel medium dries perfectly crystal clear creating sparkling, transparent textures and impastos.

Matte Gel Medium is useful when creating collages.

Heavy Gel Medium will make your acrylics have density and drag and make them look and feel more like an oil painting. This will dry with a glossy look.

Opaque Gel Medium can be mixed 50/50 with acrylic paint without changing colors since it is translucent white and high density like oils.

Texture Gels are fun to work with and are used to produce a variety of textural effects and impasto effects. They come in all different varieties such as natural sand, resin sand, ceramic stucco, black lave, blended fibers, opaque flakes, glass beads and light modeling paste. So go crazy and knock yourself out experimenting.

Modeling paste, when used wet, can be textured and carved when it dries. One would use this to create decorative molding and picture frame embellishments.

Iridescent Tinting Medium when mixed with your acrylics will make your paint iridescent.

Extender Medium when mixed with any acrylic color will make it go further and become more economical.

Retarder spray is used when you want to add to your colors to slow down your drying time.

Flow Aid when you add it to your colors will allow your paint increase the flow and workability.

Airbrush Medium when added to your colors will allow the paint to flow freer and smoother through your airbrush.

For the water color artist there are many watercolor mediums such as:

Masking Fluid which is a rubber cement-like medium used to block out white areas of the painting and it is easily removable with a rubber cement pick-up from your paper. However it is not easily removable from you rugs or most other places. Read the directions carefully.

Blending Medium will slow down your drying time.

Iridescent Medium will give your watercolor painting a glittery or pearlescent effect.

Texture Medium will contain fine particles and it will give your watercolors an impression of structure and depth.

Lifting Preparation allows you to life dry colors including staining colors from your paper.

Granulation Medium will simulate granulation of colors which do not naturally with a granulated appearance.

Ox Gall liquid is a wetting agent use to improve the flow and acceptance of watercolor paint.

Gum Arabic will increase the brilliance transparency and gloss of your watercolor painting.

Aquapasto is a translucent gel medium which will produce a thickened impasto texture.

Here is a list of Oil Painting Mediums that you should know about.

Liquin™ is used with oil paint for fine detail and glazing and will speed up drying time.

Oleopasto is an alkyd resin used with oils to produce thick, impasto work.

Win-Gel is another versatile painting medium used when you want to increase gloss and your speed drying time.

Linseed Oil is mixed with oil paint to improve flow.

Blending is a glazing medium you can use with oil paint to reduce the consistency and slow down your drying time. It is very good for blending, glazing, staining and stroke work.

Wax Medium will add translucency to your oil paintings to make them look more brilliant. This can also be used as a final coat on your **DRY** oil painting

Cobalt Dryer when added to oil paint will speed up your drying time greatly.

Rectified Turpentine should be double distilled and is used to reduce consistency of oil paint and will increase the flow.

Regular Turpentine is used to clean your brushes and palettes. Many companies have odorless versions in today's art market place thus making your studio less smelly. Grumbacher even produces Grumtine® which smells like oranges.

This should give you some idea of what you will need. You will notice that it is more expensive and time consuming to create with oils. This was basically my most serious medium in my early years of painting. Then I became too busy with life, work and family to find time to paint for many years until January of 1999. I painted several paintings in oils and then said to myself I will try some watercolors and it has been "Katie bar the Door" thereafter!

Experiment and try different things and find out what you will want to do. I am still experiments in the last 7 years and will continue to do and try different things.

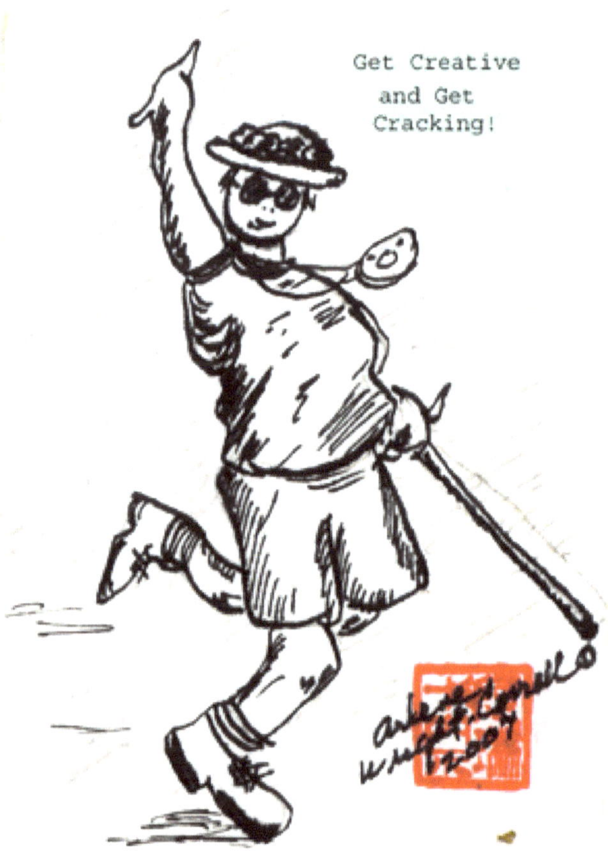

If you say why? I will answer Why Not!

Chapter 10

How to Use Your Arts and Crafts as Currency to Buy What You Need

Long before there was cash, barter was civilization's main currency. Aztec Culture was the follower of the tradition inherited by the Mayas, who a long time before, used chocolate as currency and food

Barter is often regarded as an old-fashioned means of exchange that was superseded because money is far more efficient. After all, in a monetary system an apple grower who needs shoes simply has to find a cobbler. In a pure barter system the apple grower would have to find not just any cobbler but one who happened to want apples at that time. Thus in virtually all civilizations, except the Incas, money came to play an important role.

The first people didn't buy goods from other people with money. They used barter. Barter is the exchange of personal possessions of value for other goods that you want. This kind of exchange started at the beginning of humankind and is still used today. From 9,000-6,000 B.C., livestock was often used as a unit of exchange. Later, as agriculture developed, people used crops for barter. For example, I could ask another farmer to trade a pound of apples for a pound of bananas.

At about 1200 B.C. in China, cowry shells became the first medium of exchange, or money. The cowry has served as money throughout history even to the middle of this century.

China, in 1,000 B.C., produced mock cowry shells at the end of the Stone Age. They can be thought of as the original development of metal currency. In addition, tools made of metal, like knives and spades, were also used in China as money.

B.C in my mind stands for Before Cash!

I discovered barter over 60 years ago when I traded comic books as a kid, money was scarce in the post depression years and once I had enough money to buy 1 comic book, I rarely had enough to buy a 2nd one. So swapping and trading commenced. I found I could add some "boot" which might be 1 comic book and 5 cents for two 10 cent comic books I had not read, or 1 comic book and something I had, but no longer wanted, but someone else might want, for two or perhaps 3 or more comic books.

Over the years this method expanded as I became specialized in section 1031 of the IRS code during my years as an International real estate consultant.

Now that I have retired and have gone back to painting full time, I find I have more art than cash in my old age. The ones I sell quickly I take cash for simply because cash is king! But there are ones that sit around and pile up in the studio.

So what is a gal to do? I remembered back to 1968 when we had changed our live styles, left our jobs, and started homesteading in a safer place to raise our 4 children. We were without any hospitalization at that time and had little cash when I became pregnant with our youngest daughter. We had enough to pay the hospital, but not the doctor. When he discovered I was an artist, he had me bring in a bunch of oil paintings after the delivery and he chose about 6 of them as payment in full for his services. Those paintings hung in his office from 1968 until his death a few years ago.

Another time I had a diamond encrust ladies wrist watch that was worth about $3,800.00. I never wore it as it really wasn't me. But to sell it I would be lucky to get $1,000.00. A local Italian restaurant was owned by a lady who fell in love with this watch. I traded it to her for $3,800.00 worth of pizzas and whatever else she sold. We ate at that restaurant for over 3 years!

Once we needed 3 stall showers for a property we had. We did not have the money for them. I looked up the manufacturer of the ones we wanted and I sent the owner a fax asking him to take in exchange a golf course community residential lot we had for some stall showers. That fax included full details of what I had including pictures. After about 4 days of negotiating, we did the deal. Part of the deal was we would pay the legal fees for the property transfer if he paid to have the showers delivered to us. He got a nice lot out in Arkansas and we got 12 stall showers. We only needed 3 and we were able to sell the remaining 9 within 30 days for cash!

Another time we needed a new computer and we found a small computer guy who took another golf course community lot we had out in Arkansas in exchange for a brand new color lap top. To him it simply was a matter of getting what he wanted for something he no longer wanted!

The chances of you bartering your arts and crafts for electric, telephone, mortgage payments; even arts and crafts supplies are very slim. However, you can barter them for other things you might want or need, thus freeing up a lot of your cash or getting you things you did not think you might be able to get, thus expanding your sales, getting your product out to more people for greater exposure and enhancing your lifestyle.

At a recent craft show, while walking around and talking to other displayers, I exchanged some of my herbal tea for some home made doggie biscuits that I later used as a gift.

Here are some barter tips that might prove helpful for you.

1. Make a list of what you have to barter. You have not only your finished product, but your services for new products. Should you be a good artist you can offer lessons, paintings of people's houses, children, etc. Make sure you have a sample to show them.

2. Make a list of the goods and services you think you need or might like such as a night on the town, some restaurant meals, dental work, eye glasses, baby sitting services, business cards, signs, whatever!

3. Consider joining a barter club. They are a great way to convert your arts and crafts into currency that can buy all kinds of goods and services from their members. Remember to make sure they have members near where you live. Also there may be a one time membership joining fee and if they want you bad enou they make take your product as part or that entire fee. All barter clubs charg transaction fee in cash each time you spend their currency.

4. Never underestimate the old adage, "Would you rather have something y getting than the something you have?" Also, remember, "Ask and you receive". No one is going to take you out and shoot you, they may jus

5. Remember everyone wants to say no. So get them to say no right o your question in the following manner, "Suppose I could show you a this painting you like without spending any money, is there any reason yo not listen to what I have to say?" "No" will usually be their answer. Then you could say, "My painting costs $??? And your eye glasses cost $???, my painting would look great in your home or on your office walls, so lets do a trade!"

6. Adding a little cash to your offer of a trade enhances it greatly. Let's say you really want some goods or services that cost $1,000.00, but you only have $500.00. When you consider that whatever they have is an unsold sale then usually one will consider the following offer. "I will give you $500.00 cash and your choice of $500.00 of my goods and services for your "whatever".

7. An over trade usually clinches the deal. When you really want something, you might consider "sweetening" it with an over trade of goods and services in the following manner: $150.00 painting or crafts for $100.00 worth of their goods and services. Keep remembering the old adage, "Would you rather have something you are getting than the something you have?"

8. Remember the cash and arts and crafts works both ways. Suppose someone asks you to paint something for them, say a mural. They want to pay you $500.00 because maybe that is all they have in their budget. You feel your services are worth $1,000.00. Don't walk away from this deal. Just ask them to throw in $500.00 worth of scrip or gift certificates for their goods or services. Make sure there is no "fuse" on them. A "fuse" is when something expires. Now you have your $1,000.00. You have $500.00 cash, you have $500.00 in scrip or gift certificates that you and your family can use or you can use them as gifts or you can sell these gift certificates at a discount. Better still you can trade them out for other things you may want or need.

9. If your arts and crafts include giving lessons remember that a potential customer is another artisan or craftsman who does not know what you know. Recently we took in a $150.00 painting on a $295.00 stained glass workshop. The student paid the difference of $145.00 in cash. Had we not shown interest in this artists painting nor offered the deal, we would not have had another student and we later discovered that this artist really wanted to take the workshop, but her current budget did not include the full workshop price, but it did once we took the

painting. Now the student has learned a new craft and is delighted with the results and is a repeat cash customer for tools and supplies!

10. Also this is a great way to look for new customers. Recently we needed some new roadside signs that looked jazzy and very professional. We went to the most artistic sign painting company we had in the area and exchanged a stained glass workshop for the signs. Both of us got something we could use. Plus this artist has become another repeat customer and a good friend.

11. Remember that most things you want have a wholesale value and many owners of those things have paid wholesale for them. Depending on what you are offering in your trade they may decide that it is worth the wholesale cost such as the computer guy with the lap top trade. Our lot which we no longer wanted, but could not sell because there were so many of them for sale was worth about $6,500.00 at that time. To buy the new lap top would cost us $3,800.00 cash at that time. He probably either built it or got it wholesale for less than $2,000.00 cash, but he could not buy any of those lots for $2,000.00 cash. Our lives had changed and we were never going to build on that lot.

12. Remember unless you like all your arts and crafts sitting on your shelves or hanging on your walls, you may need to get creative in marketing them. Using them to become a buyer of things will make sales happen faster than if you are just a seller!

13. One can trade wholesale for wholesale, retail for retail, wholesale for retail, retail for wholesale. Just remember these trades are sales and may be considered by the IRS as taxable so treat it as such.

14. You may even need to collect sales tax on the trades and that has to be in cash. Also anything you are going to use yourself and not resell is usually considered taxable by the sales tax department.

15. There are such services that are considered "perishable". What is a "perishable" item? An unfilled seat on an airplane, telephone time, an unused hotel room, an unsold meal, just to name a few. Could a hotel chain use your original art? Sure they can, but you will have to put some effort into it to find one. How about the small local one in your town or nearby town? Walk in with some of your art and get a nice weekend retreat for 2, or a place to put up some special guests. The same works for the local restaurants. Their walls need some dressing up, they get original art, and you get nice meals and added exposure to your art.

16. Don't be intimidated by the size of the company you are approaching. Pepsico, General Electric, Textron, Occidental Petroleum, Levi-Strauss, Control Data, McDonnell Douglas, General Motors, Massey Fergerson and Fred's Dry Cleaners have all turned to trade. The big companies have special barter divisions and the small companies will learn if you take the time to teach them. Matter of fact, the smaller companies has owners who are easier to reach than the bigger ones. These owners are the decision makers!

17. Need music lessons for your kids, or special tutoring? Talk to the teacher about taking some of your arts, crafts or services for their services. Explain to them that your arts, crafts or gift certificates for your services, i.e. lesson would make excellent gifts of any kind during the year. Explain to them that they might be able do their whole Christmas shopping through this kind of trade, thus saving their own cash for something else.

18. You never get a second chance to make a good first impression. Keep that in mind. Hold yourself out as a professional. Make your presentations professional, your business cards, have a website or some presence on the internet. Give them a place they can see your wares at. Most people will give you credit for being bigger or better than you are, for knowing more than you know when you make that good first impression. Take advantage of it!

19. Need yard work? Go and see your local landscaping firm. Offer some of your arts and crafts in exchange for 1 season of mowing and weed whacking. Explain to him that he can sell your stuff in a gift section of his store. If he doesn't have one, show him the benefits of opening one. Home and garden décor should be part of his store!

I could go on and on. You need to start thinking outside the envelope or to start thinking 360 degrees.

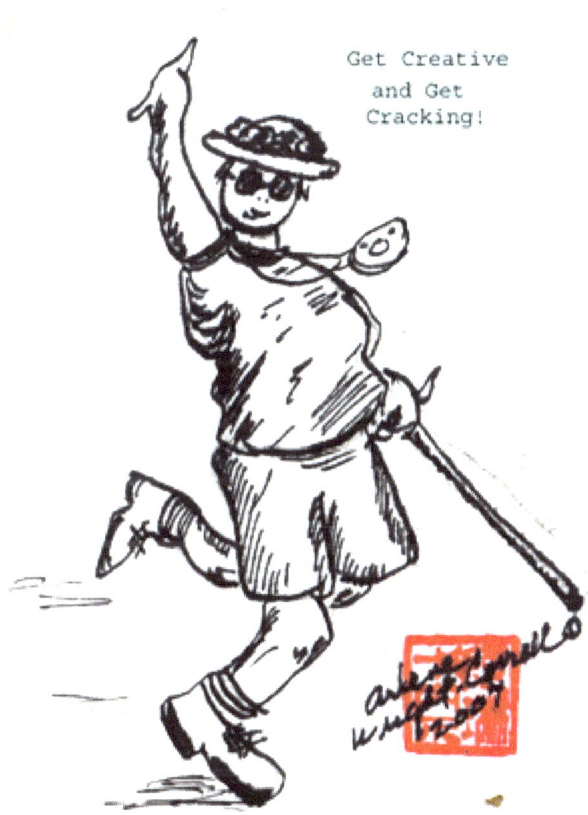

Since 9/11 the citizens of our wonderful country are finding they have less and less spendable income.

The ripple effect has spread far and wide and that affects the arts and crafts community. Each of us needs to become aware of this fact. Each of us needs to find new ways to market our arts and crafts.

Barter is just one more way to do it.

Chapter 11

"How to Expand Your Arts and Crafts Sales from Locally to Globally or How to Sell on the Internet."

In my last chapter we spoke about using barter to increase your arts and craft sales and I ended that article with the following words, "Each of us needs to find new ways to market our arts and crafts."

If you have a computer or access to a computer and you are not using it to expose your arts and crafts to millions of people on the internet, then you need to start thinking in that direction.

All of us get spam or unsolicited emails daily. I get anywhere from 800 to 1200 per day even with blockers and all kinds of good stuff. Why? Because my art work is all over the internet. I just wade through them because I get sales off the internet. I can eliminate the spam in less than 48 seconds.

Spam comes with the territory and it comes in all forms. We get plenty of "spam" in our regular mail box… Only we label it "Junk Mail"! I personally like junk mail. Why? Because some big company has spent hundreds of thousands of dollars to get the correct marketing ideas for them and most of the time the marketing will work for type of product. I get some of my best ideas from Junk Mail. It is my own inexpensive form of research and development.

I find I do not get too many great ideas from spam, but occasionally I get a lead or a link to something that will head me towards a market place that will produce a sale for me.

Most artists and craftspeople are disinclined towards marketing themselves. After almost 40 years in marketing real estate, I find that past career came in handy when I was able to devote my full time towards my art. I do not know how good my talent is, but I have sold more of my paintings while I am alive than Van Gogh ever did while he was alive! Not that I am putting myself in the same class, but who the heck wants to be famous when they are dead? Not me. I get great pleasure when one of my paintings leaves my studio and I have personally sent it to another state or another country.

However, marketing is what is needed and the cheapest form of marketing is Internet Sales.

Where can we find the right venue? Here are some things that work for me.

1. eBay. In the beginning it is very cheap. It is free to set up an eBay account. Once you have 10 sales you can open an eBay store should you wish to. You do not have to. When I opened our store it costs us a minimum of $9.98 a month. Now it costs $15.98 minimum a month.

2. I find putting things in my store front with good until sold with a make offer check is the cheapest way to expose my stuff.
3. When I put something up for auction I do not spend the money for a reserve bid, I just start my auction at the lowest I will take.
4. eBay fees have increased in the last year, so you have to say no to a lot of what they offer because sales are feast or famine, but you can control your inventory.
5. Payments are fast and secure.
6. You need a credit card on file or a bank account for direct deposits or to pay when you buy something.
7. Another bonus with eBay is when I need some art or craft supply, I look up what it costs in the store and on the internet and then I search for it on eBay. Many times I have purchased something for a fraction of the cost.
8. I get one free picture on eBay, so I have learned to use photo merge from Adobe and get all sides of a product into one free photo.

Another must for the internet is having a PayPal account. It is free to set one up and the fees are cheap, the payments are fast and they are secure.

Another site I recommend is a site called Yessy. Yessy allows you to put up your own gallery for only $5.00 per month or $59.00 per year. They have a 14 day free trail and during that time you can put up your own site/gallery complete with bio. They allow you to have as many items for sale. You earn 100% of your sales. Yessy does not charge a sales commission. If a buyer chooses to pay through the Yessy ordering system, then a low 10% payment processing fee applies. This covers credit card transaction fees and related payment processing costs. There are no other fees.

I love the ease of moving around in Yessy and I love the professionalism it gives me for only $59.00 a year. I love the site stats feature which shows how many viewers visited my gallery.

In both Easy Edit and Power Edit, there is a section entitled "Commerce" where you provide your payment information. You can pay by credit card or U.S. bank account. For a bank account, they tell you what is a routing number and account number?

They have a click here to popup an image of a routing and account number. The routing number is a 9-digit number on your check and is used to identify your specific financial institution. The account number is used to identify your bank account.

The annual fee is paid on the day your free trial ends should you wish to continue. The 10% payment processing fee is only paid when a purchase is made through the Yessy ordering system. The 10% payment processing fee is automatically removed from the purchase price and the remaining 90% is transferred to you, the seller. If the order is refunded later, then Yessy refunds the 10% payment processing fee as well.

Yessy is a privately held corporation located in Boulder, Colorado and was founded by an artist for the purpose of providing a better way to buy and sell art.

Since the beginning, the pursuit of Yessy has been to provide a wide variety of artists the opportunity to sell their art in a manner that is easy-to-use, powerful, and affordable. We believe it is more important to assist and contribute to the art community rather than focusing on financial gain. It is this philosophy that keeps any fees low, provides genuine help to artists and art buyers, and builds trust and loyalty in the art community.

Yessy is able to ease many of the difficult tasks associated with selling art, freeing artists to focus on what they love to do, creating artwork. Artist's can display their art within minutes and make it available for purchase instantly. Yessy manages the commerce aspects and automatically transfers the funds directly to the artist when their art is purchased. Yessy artists also benefit as a group, promoting art on a greater scale than is possible by an individual artist.

The enjoyment of buying art is enhanced with fast-loading and clutter-free pages, logical browsing and searching, along with the ability to instantly purchase from a large variety of art and artists. The clean, simple, and functional design of Yessy allows the focus to remain on the artwork.

There are no hidden fees with Yessy. Yessy feels it is in everyone's best interests to communicate in a clear, straight-forward, and easily understandable manner. Yessy does not believe in popup advertising, spam, or other similar tactics, and will not advertise using such methods. Yessy is technologically advanced, but there are also good values to be learned from the past.

The name Yessy is a tribute to a fellow artist from Colombia, South America who will always be remembered for her integrity and inspiration. I have sold paintings to people all over the planet from Yessy.

There are several other places such as www.USFreeads or http://www.gallery-worldwide.com . I have sold some things on USFreeads but so far nothing on Gallery-worldwide. But neither cost me anything except my time. So the exposure is there.

How much time do you need to spend on your internet marketing?

I spend anywhere from 10 minutes a day to 5 or 6 hours a week. It just depends on what I am doing. In the beginning it took me a lot of time to set these up. Really no time to maintain unless something expires.

I find that I spend upwards of 10 to 30 minutes once I make a sale. It usually takes me about 10 minutes to process all the paperwork on the net and then in the event I have only one of these items that sell, and I have it listed in several places, then I have to remove it from the other places and that may take about 20 minutes. I also have to remember where I have put my art.

Then of course we have our own website and our own domain name. Why not have yours. I struggled for years with ISP and computer guys until I finally took the reins in hand and did it myself and found a great web hosting service call www.weblogger.com

Weblogger allows me to monitor or change my site from anywhere in the world including an internet café. They have great service. I used to pay about $90.00 a month for web hosting, My Weblogger cost is about $300.00 a year which is the biggest bang for the buck around as far as I am concerned.

You can get a cheaper site somewhere, but it will not have the scope that you may want to need. A good place to check out is a site called www.goDaddy.com You can start small there and add to it as you go.

Plus you can email me and I will consider carrying your art work on our website for a modest fee. askarlene@scrtc.com

So stop fooling around and go global. I live in a town of less than 2000 people. How many sales am I going to make without the internet? Not many.

But with the sites I mentioned, I find I truly live in a global village where there are buyers with spendable dollars for my artwork.

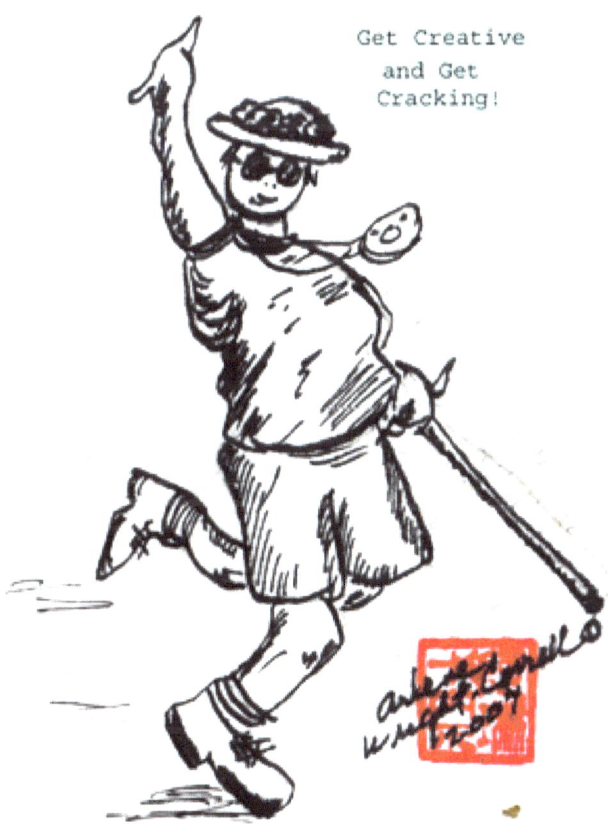

Chapter 12

How to Experiment with Encaustic Art

Encaustic paint is made from pure pigment and a mixture of molten beeswax and Damar resin. The paint is applied hot with a variety of tool, then cools and hardens within seconds. The process is quite seductive, tactile, and sultry. Painting with hot wax results in a velvety matte finish, like the frosting on a donut.

The most amazing thing about encaustic is the endless versatility. Multiple layers of paint and clear wax create overlapping color and amazing depth. The medium can be textured, scraped, incised, etched, combed, embossed, sculpted into three dimensional bits or smoothed to a glassy finish.

The molten nature of the medium just begs to be used for collaging or imbedding mixed media into the wax. Since beeswax is compatible with oil paint, oil pigment sticks can be used to glaze in rich color or to fill in incised markings.

Even though this is a new medium for me Encaustic Painting Is Older Than Oil Painting. Although it seems new, encaustic is actually one of the world's most ancient and archival painting mediums, predating oil paint.

The Fayum portraits from Grego-Roman Egypt, circa 100 B.C. to 200 A.D., have survived through the centuries. Encaustic was a lost art until pioneer Jasper Johns began contemporary encaustic painting in 1954, exposing it to a new generation of artists.

Encaustic painting requires very particular materials and equipment like heat guns, blow torches, tacking irons, crock pots and electric griddles. New tools are constantly being discovered and because this is new to me, I use items I find in hardware and kitchen supply stores, plus whatever I have around my own kitchen.

Here are some examples of my Encaustic Art experimentations. I sold 1 of them immediately within a few days of putting them on the internet.

"Poppies in the Wind"

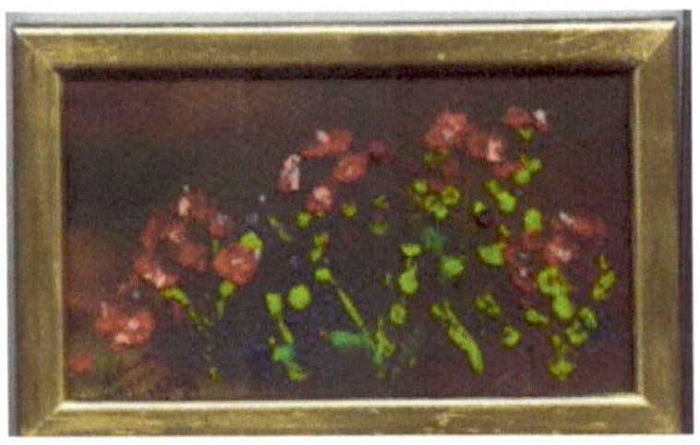

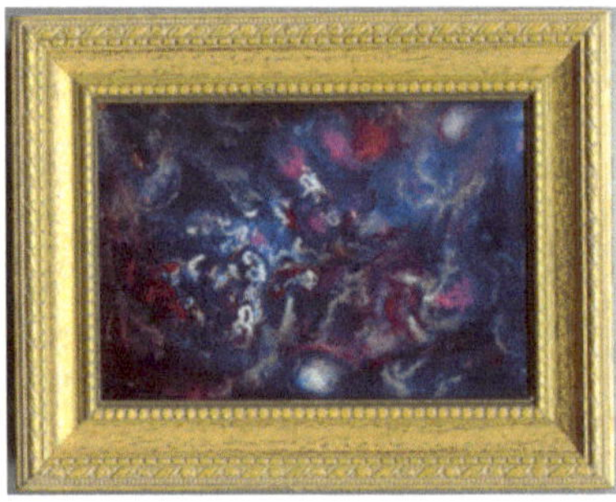

"Aurora Borealis" SOLD

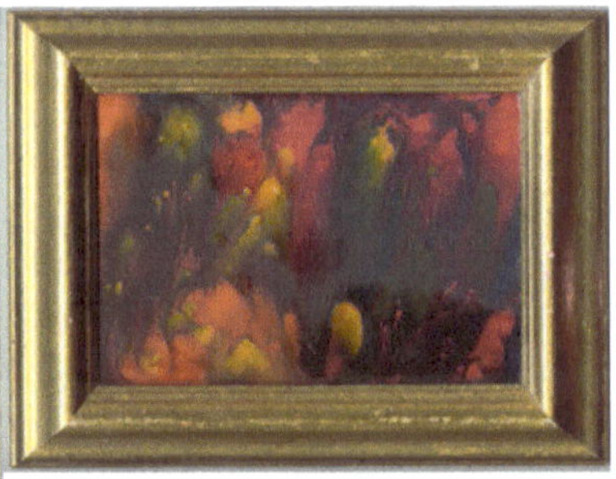

"Undersea Garden"

These were all 5 x 7" paintings done on left-over pieces of Masonite board and I use the rough side because it gives a canvas like finish to the finished piece. I buy 10 or 20 - $1.00 frames at the Mighty Dollar store in Bowling Green, KY. When Carl is getting ready to cut Masonite Board for a project I ask him to save me the leftovers and I have him cut them to fit the $1.00 frames and I stack them all on a shelf for future works of art.

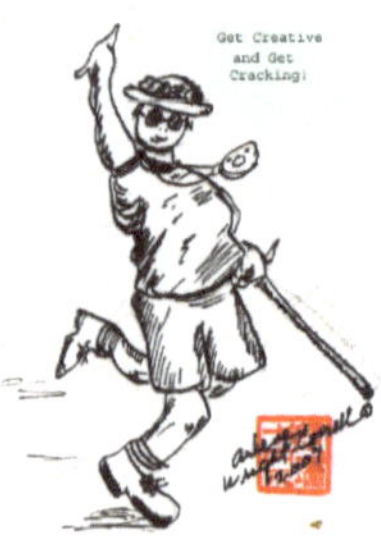

Chapter 13

How to Try Your Hand at China Painting

I met a lady at our Munfordville, KY Civil War Day's booth where we were giving a stained glass demonstration. Her name is Patty Griffin and you can read about her on my website by going to this link. http://www.learn-america.com/stories/storyReader$1909 She is one incredible China and Porcelain Painter and I discovered she lived right up the road from us. She wanted to learn stained glass making and I wanted to learn what she knew so we bartered out some lessons, materials and equipment.

This is a totally different thing here. Every layer of paint has to be put on separately and then fired in a kiln. Then the next layer etc, etc, etc!

I thought I would try something akin to pen and ink so I made this tile for my daughter Glynis as my first project. It took 5 firings. I got the pattern from a book Patti had and transferred it onto the tile with artist's transfer paper. Glynis loves undersea things and dragons and griffins. After it was done I was able to fit it into this lovely frame. I was hooked. This project, not counting the firing, took 4 three hour lessons for a total of 12 hours. Glynis was thrilled to pieces with it!

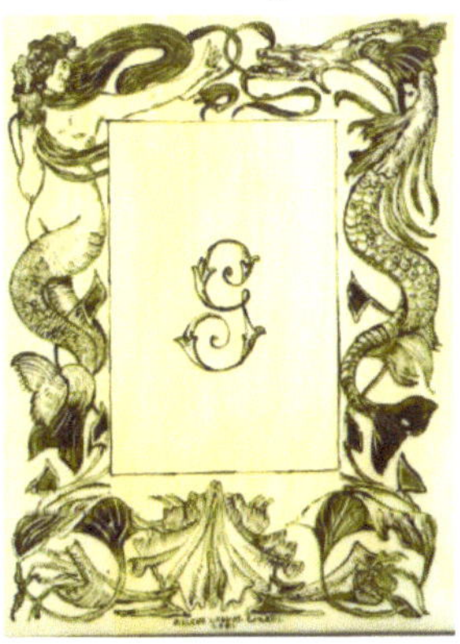

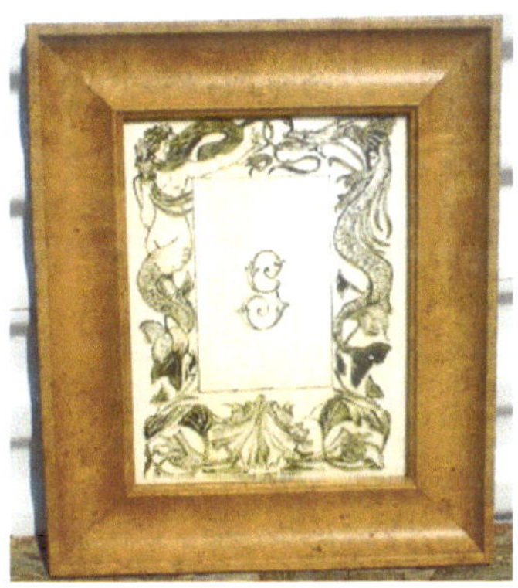

My next project was more elaborate and scary because you must develop a very light hand and light brush strokes which is often the total opposite from all the other art I had been doing. 8 firings later here is my Moss Ross Bon Bon dish. Then I decided to make Glynis a chocolate set with all different kinds of underwater fish. Our other daughter, Donna got a set with her last name initial on it so she can pass it on to her son.

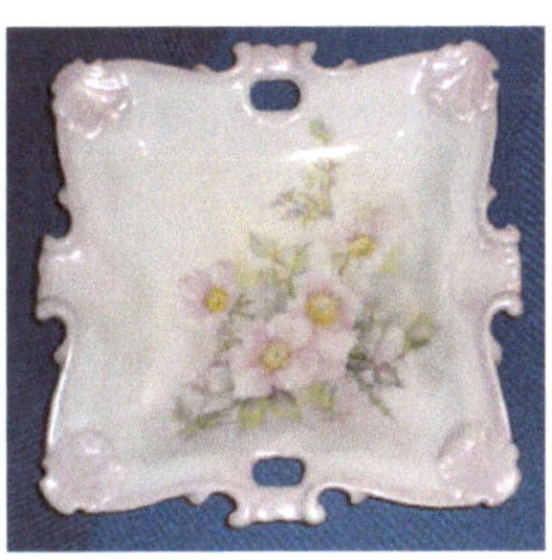

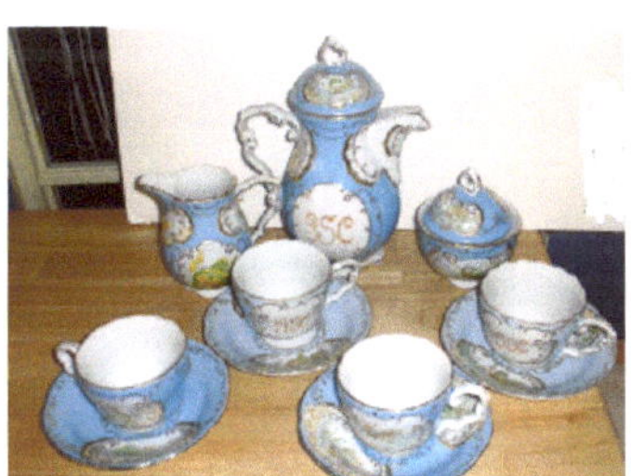

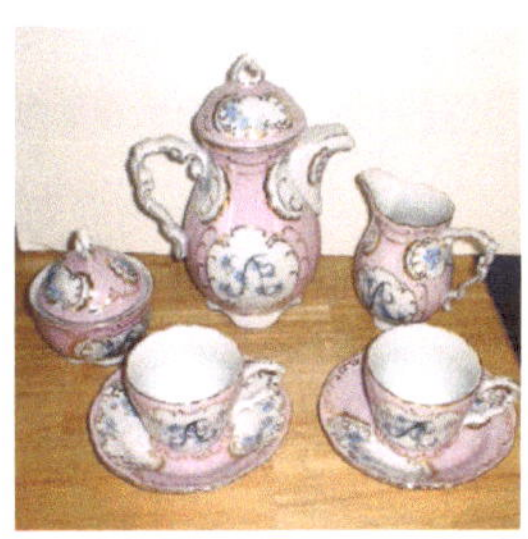

One thing lead to another and Patti came across one of her students who was not happy with

the kiln she just bought and Patti introduced me to her and I was able to get a lovely little kiln for a song and I can play with it at home at my own speed. So here are some of my experiments.

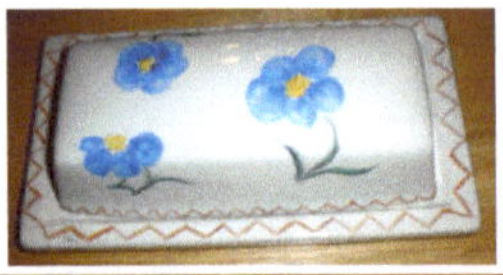

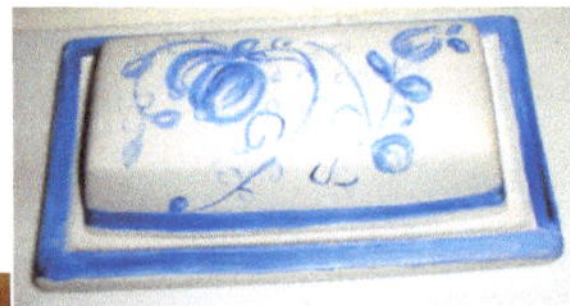

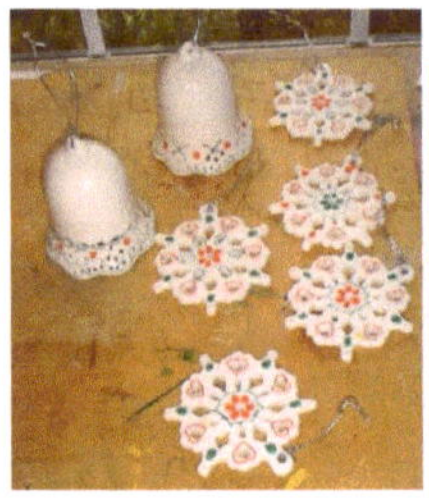

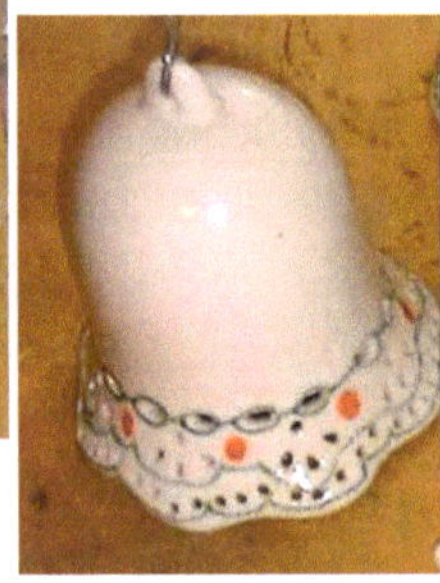

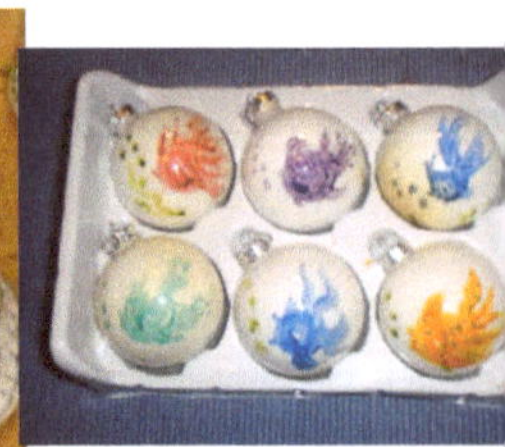

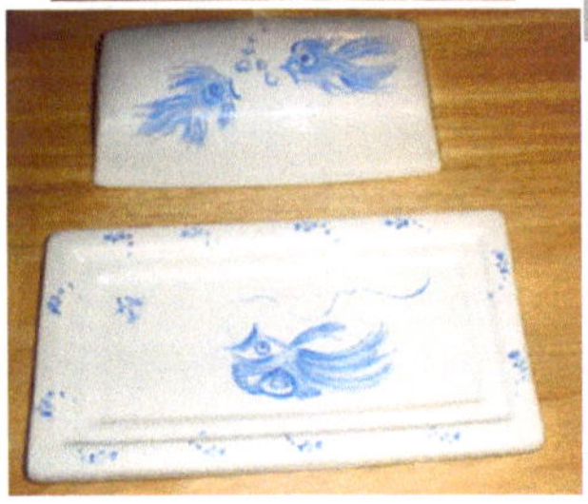

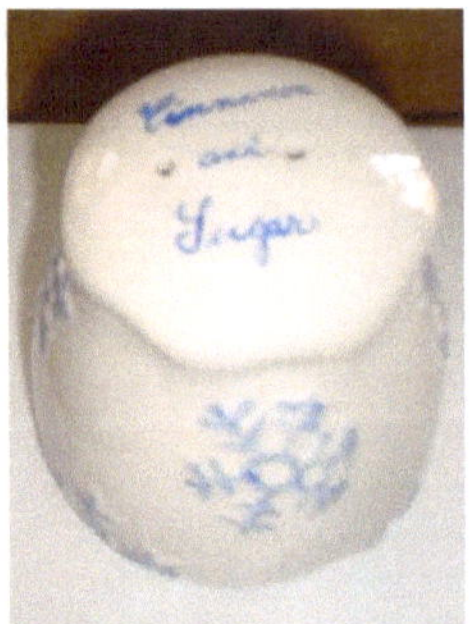

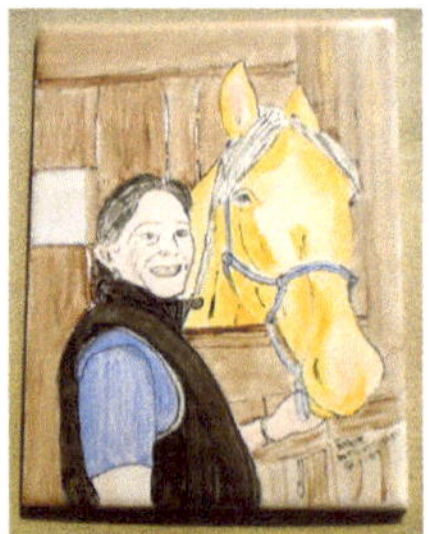

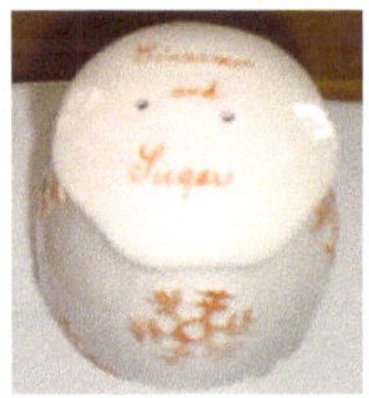

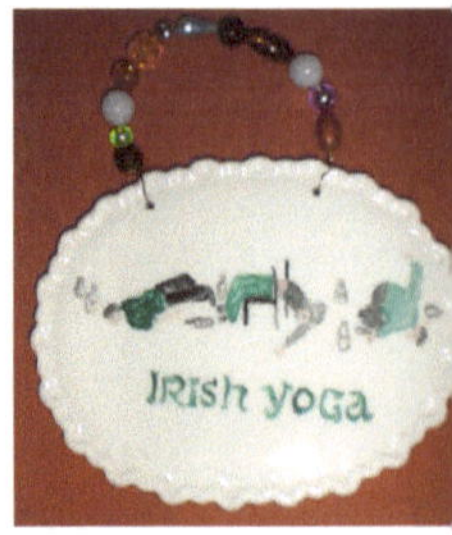

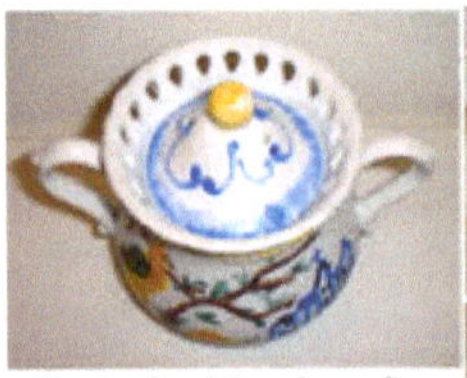

Hand painted Jam Jar or Sugar bowl by Arlene Wright-Correll "The Umbria Village"

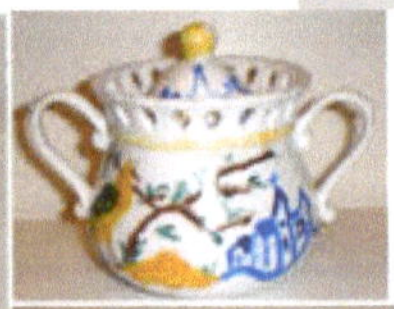

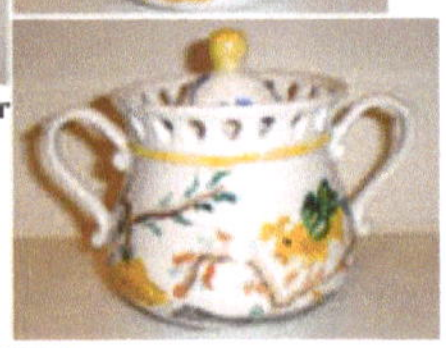

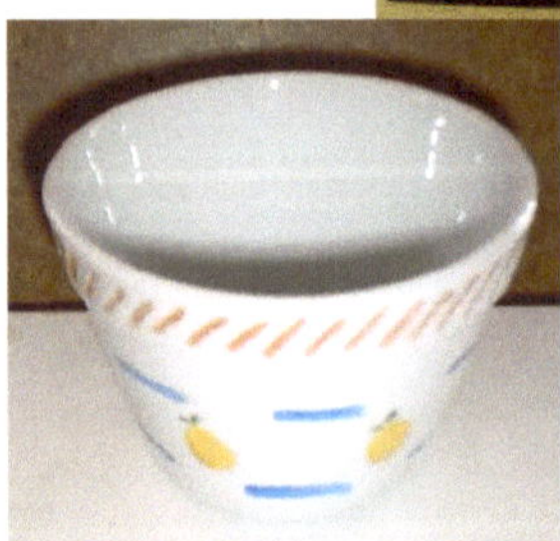

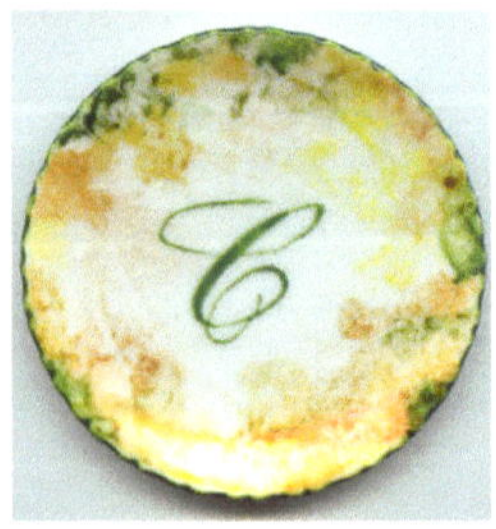

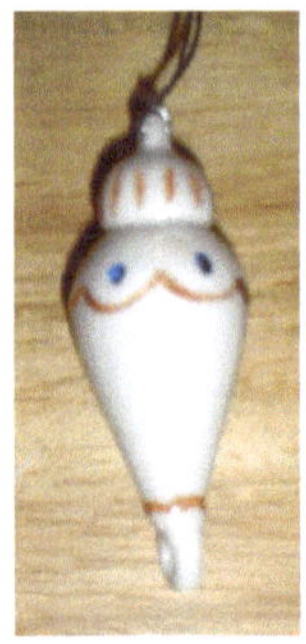

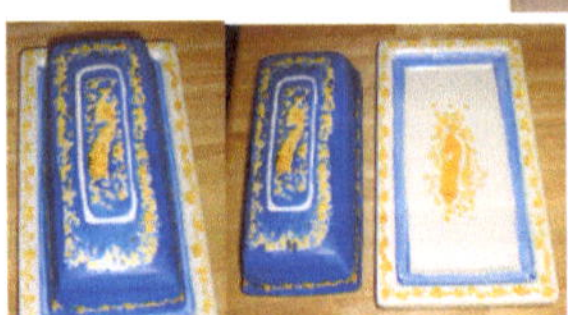

Hand Painted Butter Dish

I find I can get sales from Maryland China Co. I can find really discounted items at T.J. Maxx's discount aisle. I find white tiles at Lowe's tile section for a fraction of the China supplier's price. Light pulls cinnamon and sugar shakers, Jam Jars, Olive bowls, butter dishes, an Irish Yoga plaque for my dear friend, Kate Kenny and loads of things to sell on the net to cover the initial cost of these things that keep me out of trouble and out of the old folk's home!

I play at this when I am in the mood. It cleans up quickly and sets up quickly and I have a stand in my studio with shelves just for my china painting supplies. When I get enough for a firing I fill up the little kiln and 3 hours later they are done, but the kiln needs to slowly cool down for another 8 to 10 hours or the china will crack.

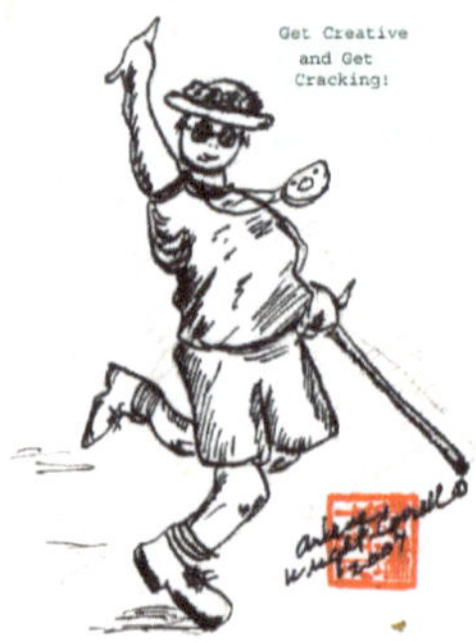

What's keeping you from trying something new and artistic?

Chapter 14

Why You Should Take Lessons from someone who knows more than you or the Art of fused and slumped glass, Egg Emulsion Painting and other good stuff

And who would that be? None other than Joe Larson and his wife Kathy Zajac and you can find out a ton of stuff about Kathy and how to do what she does by going to this website. http://www.learn-america.com/stories/storyReader$1616

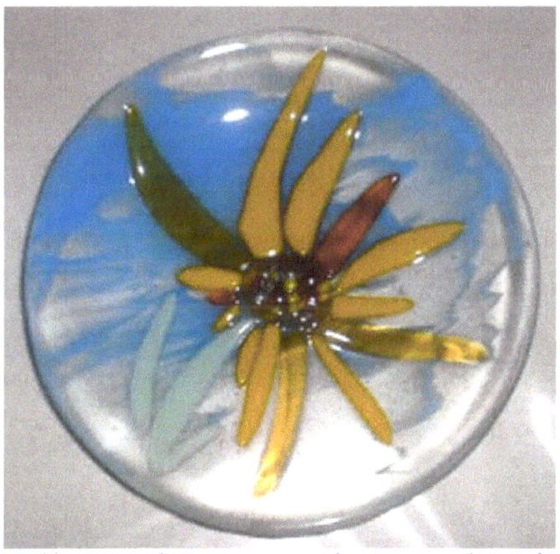

This is my first piece of fused and slumped glass. A 7.4" dish called "Sunflower" created January 8, 2007. Now that I know my little kiln can do small pieces like this I will eventually get up enough courage to try something on my own.

Then I met an incredible painter whom I became friends with. Jef Dirig and he paints water colors with egg yolk emulsion. You can find him at this link.
http://www.learn-america.com/stories/storyReader$1616

He and I put on a workshop together in 2007. I structured and advertised the workshop and he ran it and I got to attend for free. Here is my first egg emulsion work of art which I learned how to float mat from Jef also.

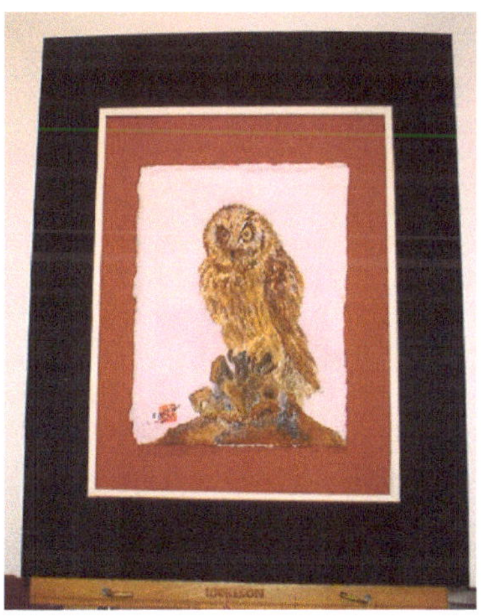

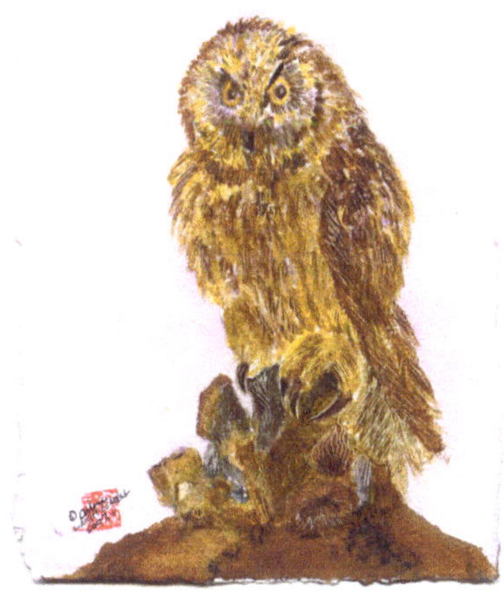

You can see what the egg yolk emulsion did to aid this painting. Our South Central Arts and Crafts Guild tries to give some sort of demonstration each month and one of our most talented artist is Donita Crain-Woodcock. She gave a linoleum wood cutting block glass one month which was a lot of fun and that lead me to experiments with wood block prints and collages. Donita's work can be seen at this link http://www.learn-america.com/stories/storyReader$1453

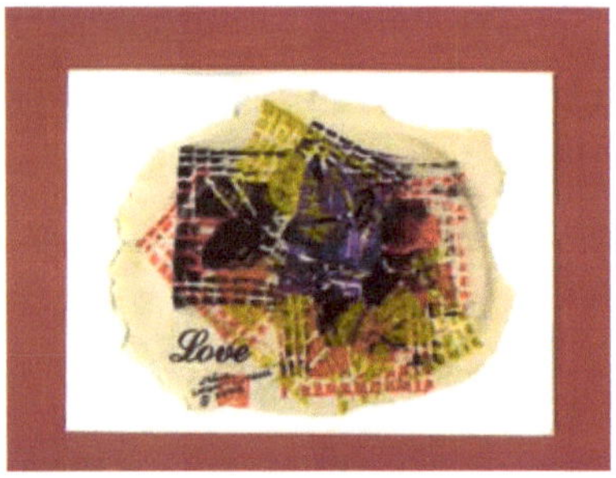

"Love Gone with the Wind"

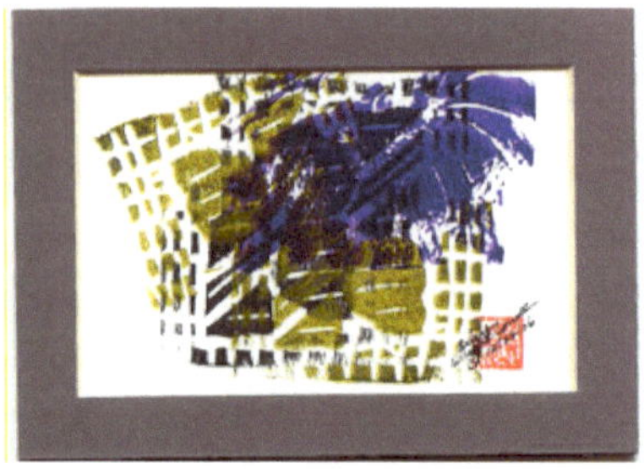

"Butterfly on Zinna"

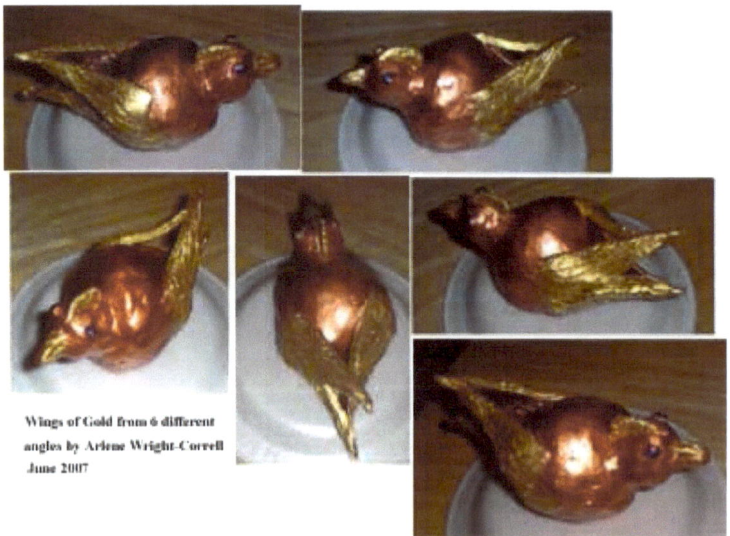

Wings of Gold from 6 different angles by Arlene Wright-Correll June 2007

Recently Donita gave a demonstration on working with air drying clay. Our project was creating a bird around a small ball of aluminum foil. We made our bird and then took it home to dry and we were to bring it back the following month to paint it with acrylic paints. Here is my bird titled, "Wings of Gold". I used copper metallic acrylic for the body, Gold metallic acrylic for the wings and glitter glue for the eyes, so I guess this is the Mixed Media Genre!

In 2006 I painted about 55 of the 77 bird houses that line the fence posts coming up our driveway into Home Farm. Even Glynis joined in the fun and made 5 of them.

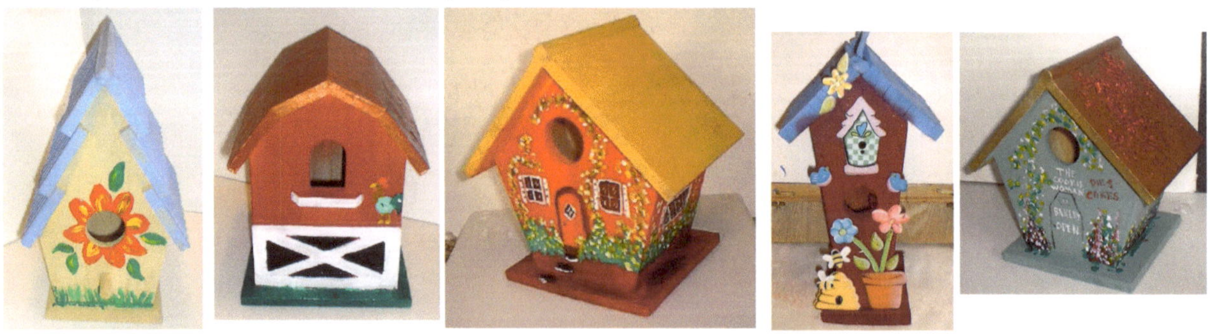

No two are alike. You can find them and more at this link. http://www.learn-america.com/stories/storyReader$1696

We wanted to learn Raku Pottery making and I found a gal over in another state that had a Raku Pottery Mobile outfit that went around and did 1 and 2 day workshops all over the place. We put one on here at Avalon Stained Glass School and had 29 enrollees.

We each made two pieces, we were able to keep one piece in our registration fee and I set up a plan for the second piece. You could either buy it for whatever you wanted $2.00 or whatever or leave it and I would auction it off and either way the proceeds would go to the National Breast Cancer Foundation. All but 5 people bought their second piece and I sold the rest. We made over $200.00 for NBCF. A win-win situation all the way around and we had a great day of networking with all these artists who came from all over with each of them never having made a Raku piece before.

Here are the pieces Carl and I made.

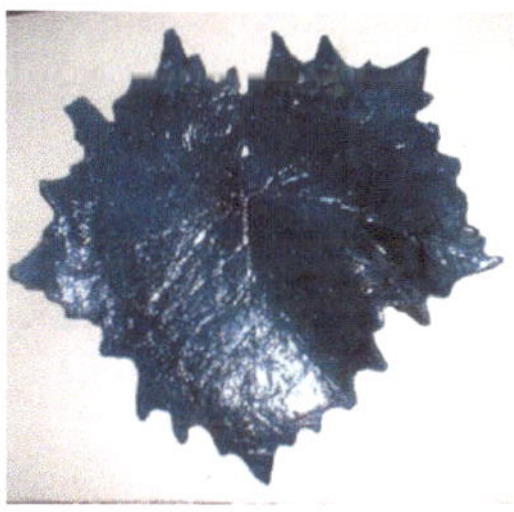

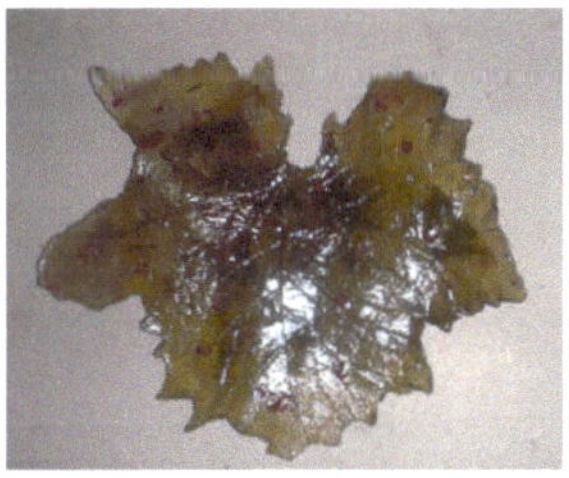

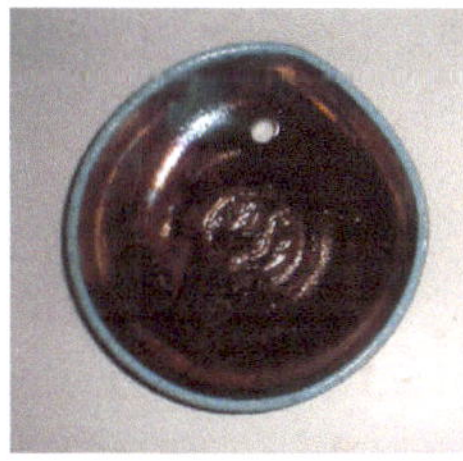

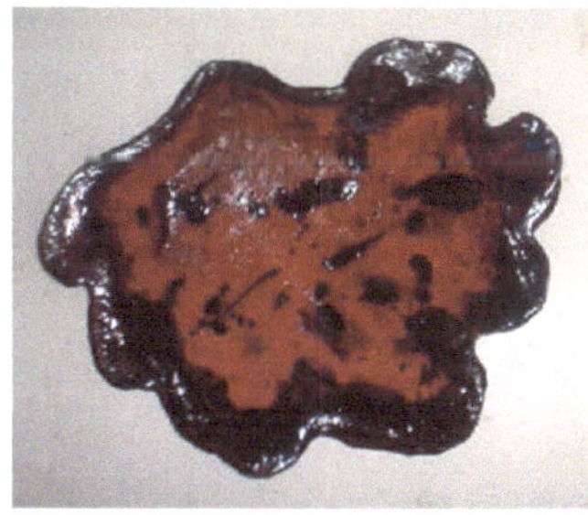

Carl's Leaf Dish   Arlene's Leaf Dish   Carl's Bowl   Arlene's Shell Dish

You can see all of the day's activities at this link and should you wish to have us bring the work shop to your town give us a call at 270 524 9567.
http://www.learn-america.com/stories/storyReader$2083

I want to learn how to do tole painting, stenciling, I want to get better and better at the things I like to do. I want to know what I don't like and never do them ever again. I am currently learning to frame my small pieces. The big pieces Carl frames for me.

I no longer do stained glass, except to create patterns such as the hand jewelry box and our Grandson Andrew fishing because my left hand is not strong since the stroke and I look like an ad for Band-Aids. But prior to the stroke here are some things I created at the first workshop we ever attended which lead Carl opening up Avalon Stained Glass School which can be seen at www.learn-america.com/stories/storyReader$134

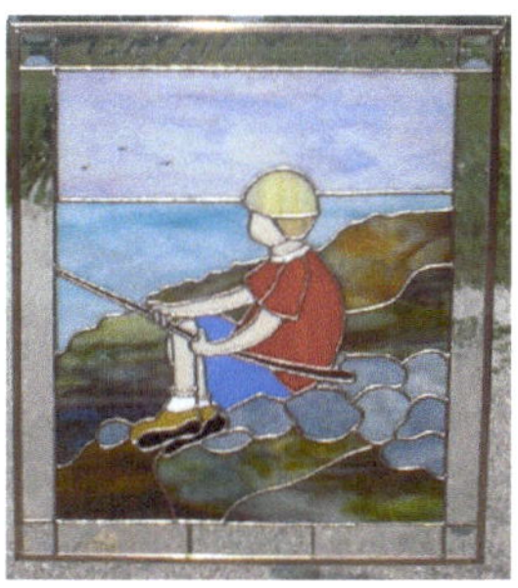

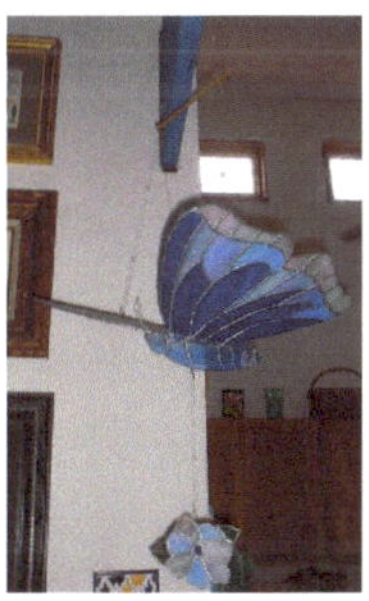

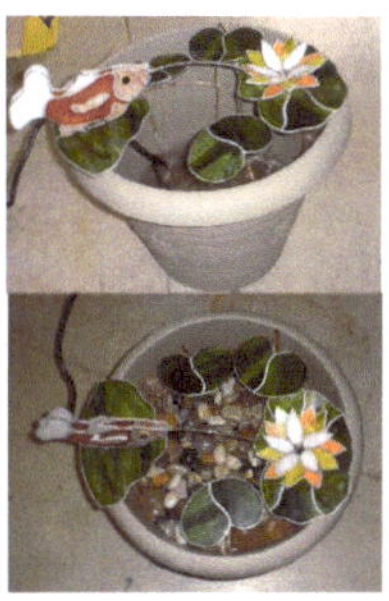

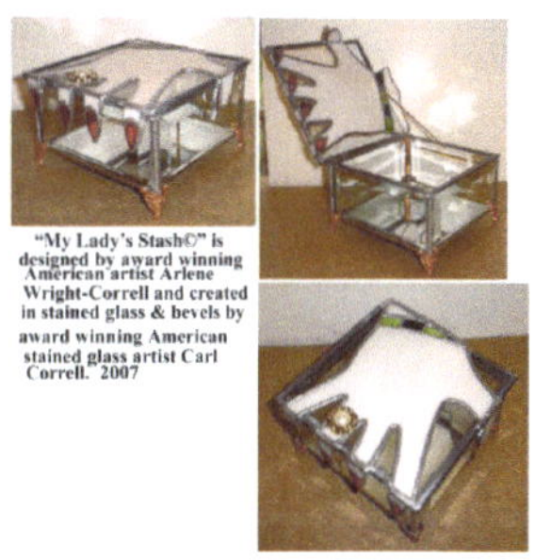

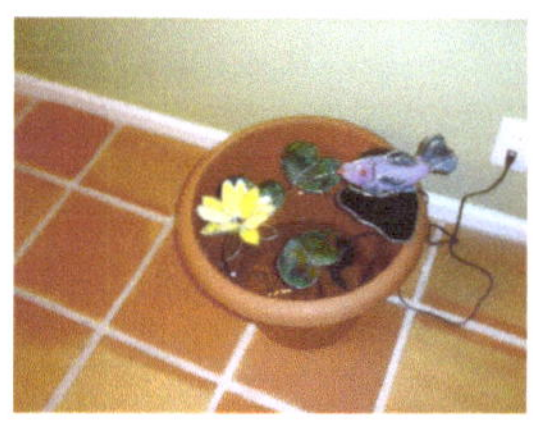

The hanging Butterfly mobile was my first project and the fish water fountains were my second and third and last projects.

Chapter 15

How to Make Your own Christmas Cards

Prior to the Christmas of 2006 I decided I would create some Half Fold Christmas cards and Christmas Post Cards. These were quite easy to do and I did them with gouache watercolor wash and upon drying I pen and inked them to completion. They now can be purchased at http://www.cafepress.com/arlene_correll/2856080 as many of my other paintings made into cards that can be framed for small art works. Here are the ones I did for that year. These were pre-sketched designs that one can get at places like Hobby Lobby and I just painted them in and then elaborated them with Pen and Ink.

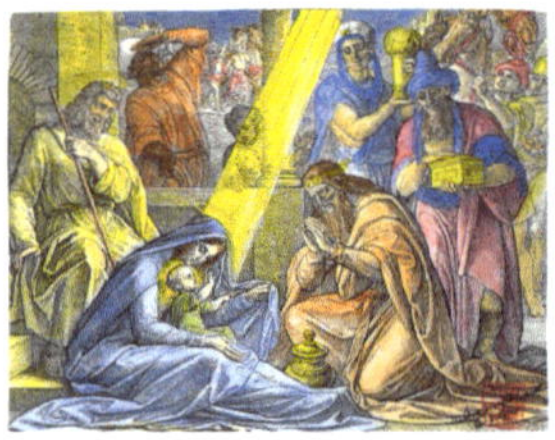

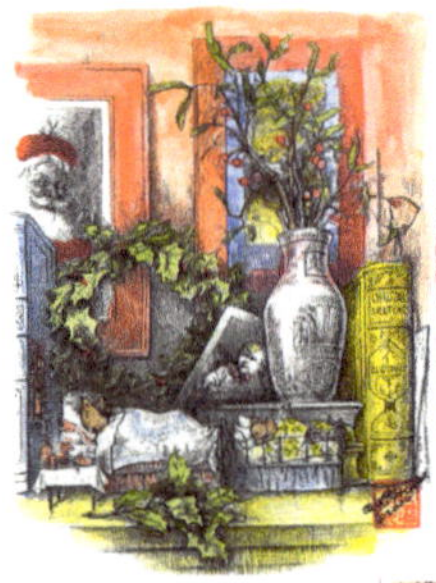

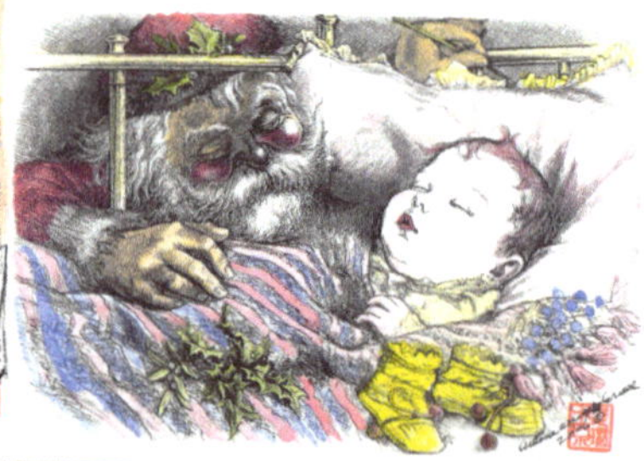

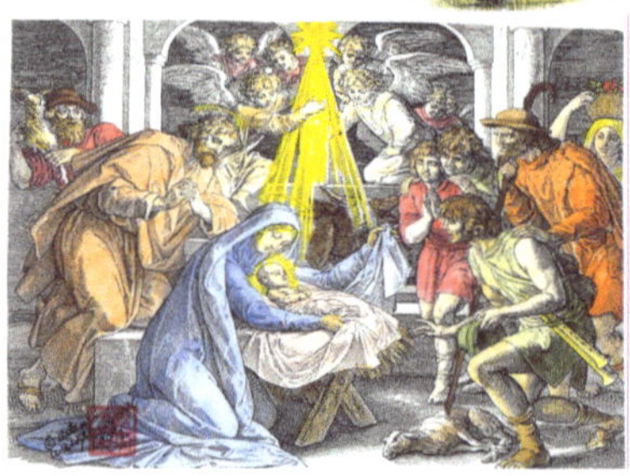

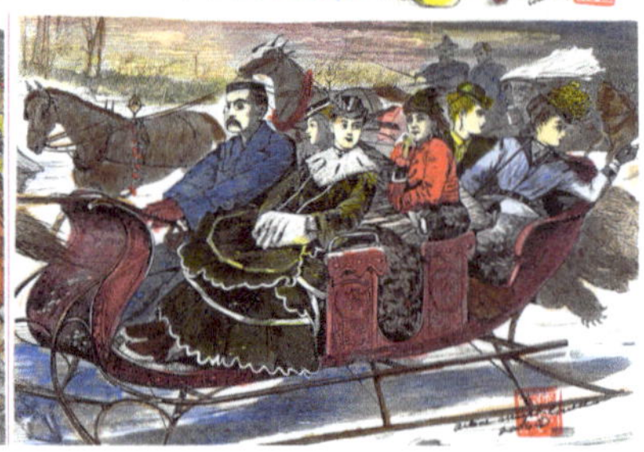

I would like to point out at this point that anyone reading this book is truly, truly capable of doing any of these things you have seen on any of these pages. Find a group in your area and join them after you find out whether they will accept novices. Just remember every one of them at one time was a novice. Go to the library and get some books, take some workshops and seminars. Heck! Come to any of my “Cheap, NO Talent Needed “3 hour workshops which includes all instructions and material for only $25.00. I guarantee you will create a frame able work of art. Or if you have a group that wants a workshop let us know and we will try to get one to you. This information can be found at http://www.learn-america.com/stories/storyReader$2044

Well, I am at the end here and perhaps I should have titled this book “Everything you wanted to know about creating your art, but were afraid to ask!”

“Tread the Earth Lightly” and in the meantime… may your day be filled with….Peace, light and love,

Arlene Wright-Correll   P.S. Get Creative and Get Cracking!